FIRST EDITION

INTRODUCTION TO
Bitcoin

David Ricardo

Introduction to Bitcoin
Ricardo, David
1b8173cdf32a38c417a5bbe279f08d951f989ae59b44ba7ae09dfd078b4fb696
Text © 2021 David Ricardo
Design © 2021 Expiscor Books
Edited by Yoshi Tanaka
88f1b2b5f3b72658c6372d945a2158a6a51f51fb5d63419eda13d85abd84d78f
Proofread by Allison Mackenzie
1c6e875d80b98cca27cab12e92dd34eb08bcf5738bad2f73242912d49d3fb15a

FIRST EDITION – MARCH 2021

LIBRARY CATALOGUING–IN–PUBLICATION DATA

Title: Introduction to Bitcoin / David Ricardo.
Other titles: Bitcoin
Names: Ricardo, David, author.
Description: Includes index and key words.
ISBN 978-1-77136-977-0 (hardcover). –
ISBN 978-1-7776923-0-8 (paperback). –
ISBN 978-1-7776923-1-5 (epub). –
ISBN 978-1-7776923-2-2 (PDF). –
Subjects: LCSH: Bitcoin.

 **EXPISCOR BOOKS**

Contact the Author:
The only way to contact me is to leave a comment in the review section on any Amazon website. I acknowledge that the subject matter of *Introduction to Bitcoin* is complex, and that I might have made errors in my explanations. I would be greatful if readers could jot down any constructive feedback and leave it in the review section on Amazon. I would also love to hear what aspects of this book you found useful or entertaining (these stories are what fuel me as a writer). I will read all comments, and will update future editions of this book based on your feedback.

Text set in Berkeley Medium. Chapter headings set in Source Sans Pro Bold.

NOTE: Bitcoin is capitalized when referring to the protocol, and lowercase when referring to spendable units of bitcoin.

CONTENTS

What Is Bitcoin?

Bitcoins were first created by Satoshi Nakamoto in 2009. They are digital coins that are used to make purchases. Every day, bitcoins trade hands online, in stores, and at Bitcoin ATMs. Bitcoin transactions can be sent through an internet connection, shortwave radio, or through satellites. They are transferred from one wallet to another without the need for a third party, such as a bank. No approval is needed to open a Bitcoin wallet, and accounts cannot be frozen. The Bitcoin software is **open source**, which means that anyone can review the code.

What Is a Cryptocurrency?

A cryptocurrency is a form of currency that only exists in digital form. Cryptocurrencies rely on the practice of cryptography to prevent fraud and **counterfeit** transactions. Cryptography is derived from the Greek word *Kryptos,* which means something that is hidden. Cryptography is used to encode and decode sensitive information in cryptocurrencies. This coding is often used to control the creation of digital units, facilitate secure transactions, and verify the authenticity of transactions.

The Four Pillars of Bitcoin

Bitcoin's software has four key components that are equally important in making the currency function. The first is a peer-to-peer network that allows anybody to take part in the process of approving transactions. This spreads out the control of authority from one central source to people across the globe. Secondly, Bitcoin has a set of rules called consensus rules. These rules allow new bitcoin to be created at a predictable rate, and are used by the peer-to-peer network in validating transactions.

Cryptography often uses mathematic principles to encode and decode messages. This practice began with the invention of the telegraph in 1844.

Thirdly, Bitcoin compiles a public record of every transaction in a **blockchain**. This establishes trust in the system, as peers can easily review the accuracy of any transaction. Fourthly, Bitcoin implements a proof-of-work mechanism that causes energy expenditure when creating blocks in the blockchain. Expended energy creates security for every bitcoin transaction, as confirmed blocks cannot be erased without a significant expenditure of energy from an attacker. These four components create a secure network that no one has been able to compromise since Bitcoin was first created. To grasp how and why theses processes function, and why they are vital for the success of the Bitcoin ecosystem, it is necessary to understand how money has evolved throughout history.

Bitcoin transmitted over radio signals can be sent to a location up to 373 miles (600 kilometers) away.

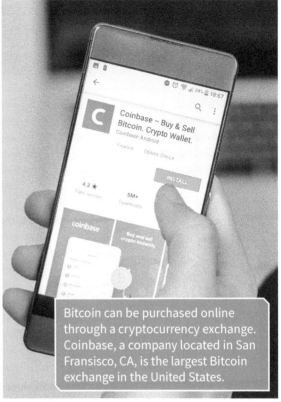

Bitcoin can be purchased online through a cryptocurrency exchange. Coinbase, a company located in San Fransisco, CA, is the largest Bitcoin exchange in the United States.

With the use of a computer and an 18-inch (45-centimeter) satellite dish, bitcoin can be sent without an internet connection. Satellites in space can receive and send these transactions across approximately 66 percent of Earth's surface.

People can trade bitcoin for cash at more than 5,000 Bitcoin ATMs around the globe.

The Evolution of Money

Money has existed in various forms for thousands of years. In ancient times, people regularly traded different types of goods and services in a system known as bartering. In this system, services or goods were traded for other services or goods without the use of a currency. In 6,000 BC, livestock and crops were often used as units of exchange. One sheep could be traded for a certain amount of wheat or several hours of labor.

The barter system was used throughout the world for thousands of years. Over time, bartering grew complicated and impractical for three main reasons. Firstly, bartering depends on a coincidence of wants. It is not always possible to find someone who is willing to exchange a particular good or service. Secondly, there is no common measure when trading goods and services. This often results in one party receiving a better deal in a trade. Thirdly, many goods and services are not easily divisible. Buying several different items can prove difficult if a buyer has only one cow to trade. To make the purchase of goods easier, people gradually agreed on a unified method of payment, called a currency, to value products and services.

The Silk Road was a network of trade routes famous for connecting Eastern and Western civilizations for the purposes of bartering and exchange. From about 114 BC to 1450 AD, people used this network to trade items such as horses, herbs, wool, and silk.

Early Forms of Currencies

In different locations around the world, early currencies took the form of beads, shells, tools, feathers, and rocks. These objects were either difficult to find or difficult to manufacture, or both. This created a limited supply, resulting in the objects becoming a store of value. Valuable objects allowed early humans to cooperate in ways not observed in any other species. Thousands of years ago, a craftsman could exchange several arrowheads for a portion of a hunter's kill. Arrowheads were therefore a tool and a collectable that could be useful as a medium of exchange.

For an object to be considered an exchangeable collectable, it usually had three properties. Firstly, an object was generally small, and easily carried. This made the collectable secure from loss or theft. Secondly, a collectable was hard to find or manufacture, which helped to create a store of value. Thirdly, an object's value could be easily measured by simple observation. An arrowhead would not need a lengthy inspection for a hunter to evaluate its worth.

Bronze arrowhead money originated near the Black Sea. Bronze money was eventually shaped into objects such as dolphins and fish before eventually being made into round coins.

What Is Shell Money?

For more than 1,000 years, hundreds of Indigenous groups in North America used clam shells for ceremonial purposes and as a currency. The shells were shaped into beads called wampum and strung onto a string. In the early 17th century, British settlers in North America lacked a sufficient supply of gold and silver coins to use as a currency. Over time, the **colonists** began eagerly trading wampum for goods and services. This led to wampum becoming legal tender in New England between 1637 and 1661. This period in history is where the term "shelling-out" originates.

When the colonists first started trading in wampum, the currency was scarce as it was difficult to make with Indigenous stone tools. However, Europeans soon applied western manufacturing techniques, producing wampums at a rapid pace. This caused **inflation**, and played a role in the British shipping in enough gold and silver coinage to support the colonists. Today, wampum has become an example of the dangers in using a currency that could be mass produced.

Gold and Silver Currencies

The use of silver and gold coins as a type of currency arose in Asian kingdom of Lydia in approximately 700 BC. Since silver and gold were difficult to mine and were highly prized for their use in jewelry, the metals were easily tradable. The use of coins as a means of transaction rapidly spread to many countries around the world, dominating older forms of currencies.

Gold and silver mining was generally a slow process, and newly mined metals would not significantly affect the purchasing price of gold. A significant exception occurred between the 16th and 18th centuries when the Spanish Empire mined more than 150,000 tons (136,078 metric tons) of silver in the Americas. This amounted to approximately 80 percent of the world's supply of silver. Spain became the richest country in Europe,

In 1603, the Spanish had more than 85,000 people mining silver at Potosí, where modern-day Bolivia is located.

while other nations saw the value of their silver treasuries plummet. Europeans who held silver also saw the buying power of their savings diminish with every boatload of silver brought from the Americas.

When Alexander the Great conquered Persia, Egypt, and India, he melted plundered gold and silver objects into coins. By 323 BC, this increase in the supply of money created a thriving economy throughout the region.

During Germany's hyperinflation of 1923, a wheelbarrow filled with German Marks could not even buy a newspaper. The currency's value was so diminished that people fashioned kites from it.

Paper Currencies

Paper money was developed as a means of making payments without the need to carry heavy coins. It was first introduced in China in 806 AD as letters of credit. Later, central banks in different parts of the world printed paper money that was backed by gold stored in vaults. However, when many governments encountered financial troubles, they resorted to printing more money. This money was either backed by the same amount of gold as before, or by a written guarantee from the government that the paper notes held value. However, history has demonstrated that governments will overprint currencies when times are desperate. During the American Civil War, overprinting of the Confederate currency caused it to suffer an inflation rate of more than 5,000 percent. After World War I, Germany issued 496.5 quintillion Marks to pay war **reparations**, dropping the currency's buying power to one-trillionth of its former value in 1914.

The value of gold, silver, and paper currencies rely on trust that various factors do not cause the total supply to rise too sharply.

Throughout history, these currencies have created periods of stability marked by periods of slow or fast corrections. Despite this predictable flaw, physical currencies share one unifying principle: they are methods of payment that can be used in face-to-face transactions that do not require a third-party to complete a transaction. This principle worked well for hundreds of years, until the advent of credit cards and the internet.

Quote from Satoshi Nakamoto

"The root problem with conventional currency is all the trust that's required to make it work. The central bank must be trusted not to debase the currency, but the history of fiat currencies is full of breaches of that trust. Banks must be trusted to hold our money and transfer it electronically, but they lend it out in waves of credit bubbles with barely a fraction in reserve. We have to trust them with our privacy, trust them not to let identity thieves drain our accounts. Their massive overhead costs make micropayments impossible."

February 11, 2009

The Creation of Internet Money

In 1969, the Advanced Research Projects Agency Network (ARPANET) established digital communication between four universities. The first message was sent over ARPANET from a computer at the University of Los Angeles to a computer at Stanford Research Institute on October 29, 1969. Over time, the computer network grew into what is known today as the internet.

While the internet connected people instantly from one side of Earth to the other, mass adoption would not occur without the framework of the World Wide Web established by Tim Berners-Lee in 1991. When Berners-Lee launched the first website, he envisioned a space where information on websites could be universally accessed by anyone. It was only a matter of time before people began to use websites as a marketplace to buy and sell items.

The first secure internet purchase occurred on August 1, 1994, when Dan Kohn sold a Sting CD on his newly created website NetMarket.com for $12.48 plus shipping to Phil Brandenberger. Unlike a face-to-face transaction, Brandenberger used a third-party to complete his payment through the use of a credit card. Brandenberger also used an email **encryption** software called Pretty Good Privacy (PGP) to securely send his credit card number to NetMarket.com.

While the transaction successfully avoided being intercepted by a hacker, using a credit card still meant that Brandenberger's card information would be seen by four participants. This included the merchant, the merchant's bank, the bank that issued

PGP was created by Phil Zimmermann in 1991. He called Brandenberger's 1994 transaction an important step towards the creation of digital cash.

the credit card, and the credit card company such as Visa or MasterCard. Brandenberger – and everyone that uses credit cards – must trust that their information will be secure with each participant. Transactions can also be declined for several reasons, including unusual purchase activity, international purchases, or if an unusual shipping address is used. Brandenberger's transaction demonstrated that there would be a demand for a trusted form of internet money that would give buyers the ability to approve their own transactions.

Internet transactions that rely on credit card payments leave out approximately **2 billion** unbanked people in the world who do not have access to credit cards.

PGP can create an encryption key that is up to **512 characters** long, making it one of the most widely used email encryption programs in the world.

The World Wide Web contains approximately **2 billion** websites.

Cyberbucks

In the early 1990s, a **cryptographer** named David Chaum was designing plans for an encryption-based currency that could be used on the internet without having to trust private information to a third party. In July 1994, Chaum's company, Digicash, offered the first 10,000 applicants 100 free cyberbucks. Each recipient of cyberbucks could freely transfer the electronic currency to others online. Transactions were secured by Blind Signature Technology, which ensured the complete privacy of users.

Blind Signature Technology worked similarly to someone placing an **anonymous** voting card inside an envelope on election day, with their personal information on the outside of the envelope. In this scenario, an election official could verify the name of the voter and use a star patterned hole-punch to make a distinct hole in the envelope and the voting card. The election official effectively placed an official signature on both documents without having to see the voting card. The anonymous voting card could then be removed from the envelope and placed inside a bin with everyone else's anonymously verified votes.

David Chaum is credited as the inventor of digital currencies for his 1982 paper, *Blind Signatures For Untraceable Payments*.

Instead of sending out personal information, Digicash users had unique strings of numbers and letters known as keys. Digicash's **server** would anonymously verify the keys of each cyberbuck transaction without knowing the contents of the transaction itself. Once approved by Digicash, the recipient of the transaction would receive their cyberbucks.

The Digicash Network

Buying items with cyberbucks originated with a consumer downloading a digital wallet from Digicash. The wallet held the consumer's public and private keys. The consumer could then use the Digicash network to purchase and spend cyberbucks.

Digicash Server

Merchant

4. Merchant transfers cyberbucks transaction

5. Digicash verifies transaction and credits merchant's account

6. Merchant ships product

1. Consumer buys cyberbucks

2. Digicash sends cyberbucks

3. Consumer buys product with cyberbucks

Consumer

E-cash Experiments

Even though cyberbucks had no **commodity** value, to **cypherpunks**, the tokens presented an opportunity to experiment with digital money. In the summer of 1995, computer scientist Hal Finney offered cyberbucks to the first person who could crack his coding contest. That same summer, cryptographer Adam Back was the first person to sell merchandise for cyberbucks in the form of cryptographically themed t-shirts. For the first time in history, internet money was being used to exchange goods.

On July 30, 1995, Ecash Exchange Market opened, allowing users to trade their cyberbucks for U.S. dollars. The exchange offered a rate of $0.05 for 1 cyberbuck.

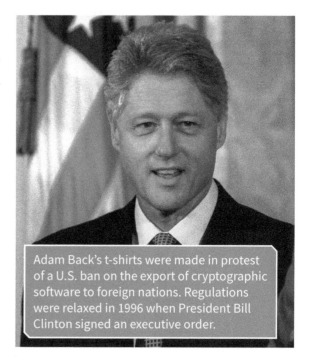

Adam Back's t-shirts were made in protest of a U.S. ban on the export of cryptographic software to foreign nations. Regulations were relaxed in 1996 when President Bill Clinton signed an executive order.

What Is a Cypherpunks?

A cypherpunk is someone who uses cryptography to encrypt messages while keeping the identity of senders and recipients private. Cypherpunks use these techniques to help enact political or social change. Cypherpunks had their origins in 1992 when a small group of cryptographers held monthly meetings in San Francisco, CA.

That same year, one of the group's founders, Eric Hughes, formed the cypherpunk mailing list. Discussions covered a number of topics including cryptography, politics, philosophy, mathematics, and computer science. The group believed that the government and corporations would erode the privacy of individuals over time, and that cypherpunks were needed to help defend this privacy. Members of the mailing list are responsible for building an anonymous web surfing project called Tor, PGP email encryption software, and early forms of electronic currencies that led to the creation of Bitcoin. The person or people behind the **pseudonym** Satoshi Nakamoto, are also believed to be members.

Decentralized Currencies

With early electronic curriencies, cypherpunks faced the problem of users double-spending when a centralized authority was removed from a transaction. Without a centralized validator, a user could cheat the system by sending the same internet money to two people at the same time. Duplicating an electronic currency in order to spend it more than once would lead to inflation and a lack of trust in the currency. Experts at the time were hopeful that a **decentralized** solution could be found. In the late 1990s, the Nobel Prize winning economist, Milton Friedman, theorized that a reliable e-cash would soon be developed. Cryptographers began searching for a reliable e-cash, with a decentralized way to validate transactions without the possibility of a double-spend occurring.

After a 3-year trial, only about 5,000 customers had signed up with Digicash. At the time, internet consumers were comfortable using credit cards despite the privacy concerns of cypherpunks.

With 1 million cyberbucks in circulation, the market valuation was $50,000. However, even though cyberbucks were slowly gaining traction among users, Digicash ran out of money to remain in business. When the company turned off its server in 1998, Digicash transactions could no longer be verified, and the currency became useless.

While Digicash proved that anonymity could be achieved, it also demonstrated to cypherpunks that a **centralized** currency was prone to failure. Cyberbucks relied on the long-term survival of Digicash to operate its server indefinitely. Going forward, cypherpunks were unlikely to place trust in a new digital currency that was controlled by one centralized authority.

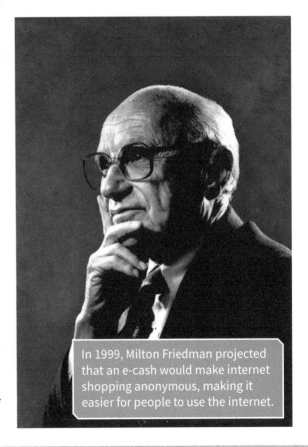

In 1999, Milton Friedman projected that an e-cash would make internet shopping anonymous, making it easier for people to use the internet.

In 2014, Bitcoin was made illegal in Bangladesh. Anyone caught using the cryptocurrency faces up to 12 years in prison.

B-money

In 1998, computer scientist Wei Dai came up with an idea for a decentralized currency called b-money. With each transaction, Dai proposed that every computer in the b-money network would credit a recipient's account and debit the account of the sender. This effectively created a peer-to-peer system, where each peer, or computer, involved in the network would help to validate the transaction in a decentralized way.

However, Dai realized that a bad-actor could cheat the system. Alice could send identical b-money units to Bob and Carol at the same time. If Bob and Carol were located in different parts of the network, peers near Bob would verify the transaction, and peers near Carol would do the same. Before all peers in the network realized that a double-spend had occurred, Bob and Carol, trusting their nearby peers, may have completed their transaction with Alice.

To stop a double-spend from happening, Dai proposed that several users would maintain servers that would record all peer-to-peer consensus in the network. Before Bob and Carol completed their transaction with Alice, Bob and Carol would check with these servers to validate the transaction. This effectively removed the possibility of Alice double-spending b-money, but it still relied on a semi-centralized network. If the people running the servers joined forces, they could double-spend at the same time. Also, governments could make the currency illegal and physically shut down each server. While b-money was never tested in the real world, its peer-to-peer consensus model would form the basis for a fully decentralized currency 10 years later.

Quote from Satoshi Nakamoto

"A lot of people automatically dismiss e-currency as a lost cause because of all the companies that failed since the 1990s. I hope it's obvious it was only the centrally controlled nature of those systems that doomed them. I think this is the first time we're trying a decentralized, non-trust-based system."

February 15, 2009

A Peer-to-Peer Network

On October 31, 2008, Satoshi Nakamoto published his whitepaper, *Bitcoin: A Peer-to-Peer Electronic Cash System* (see Appendix). In the document, Nakamoto described the full details of a completely decentralized currency. Unlike credit cards, Digicash, and all prior forms of electronic payments, Nakamoto had found a way to solve double-spending while also removing centralized validators from the approval process.

Nakamoto's solution was a universal **ledger**, known as a blockchain. Similarly to an accountant's ledger, the blockchain keeps a record of every bitcoin transaction in history. Approximately every 10 minutes, a new group of transactions, grouped into a block, is added to the blockchain. To validate each block, Bitcoin follows a similar peer-to-peer consensus mechanism as b-money. Unlike b-money, users of Bitcoin would not be required to trust a semi-centralized network of validators to stop double-spending.

Double-Spending

Bitcoin solves double-spending by only allowing one double-spent transaction into a block. If Alice sends the same 0.5 bitcoin units to Bob and Carol, both transactions would go into a pool of unconfirmed transactions. Different peers in the network would pull Bob and Carol's unconfirmed transactions from the pool and independently validate that the 0.5 bitcoin units came from Alice. If a peer sees Alice's transactions to Bob and Carol, the peer will discard both transactions.

Some peers in the network may only see one of Alice's transactions. These peers would validate Alice's single transaction, and add it to the most current block in the blockchain. All future blocks in the blockchain would not accept Alice's second transaction. In this way, either Bob or Carol will receive a validated transaction from Alice, but not both. If Bob received confirmation from the network, his possession of Alice's 0.5 bitcoin will be recorded on the blockchain.

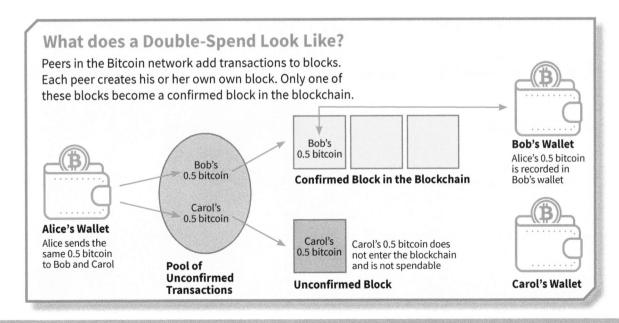

What does a Double-Spend Look Like?

Peers in the Bitcoin network add transactions to blocks. Each peer creates his or her own own block. Only one of these blocks become a confirmed block in the blockchain.

Alice's Wallet
Alice sends the same 0.5 bitcoin to Bob and Carol

Pool of Unconfirmed Transactions
Bob's 0.5 bitcoin
Carol's 0.5 bitcoin

Bob's 0.5 bitcoin
Confirmed Block in the Blockchain

Bob's Wallet
Alice's 0.5 bitcoin is recorded in Bob's wallet

Carol's 0.5 bitcoin
Carol's 0.5 bitcoin does not enter the blockchain and is not spendable
Unconfirmed Block

Carol's Wallet

Transparency

Recording transactions on the blockchain creates a layer of security that everyone in the network is able to see. Transactions are recorded using cryptographic public and private keys that were similarly used by Digicash in 1994. A private key is a randomly generated number, and a public key can be mathematically calculated from that private key. However, a public key cannot be used to decipher a private key. In Bob and Carol's transaction, each would have sent their public keys to Alice. To see their transactions with Alice, Bob and Carol would search for a recording of their public keys on the blockchain using a block explorer website, such as blockexplorer. com. When Carol searches for her public key, she will see that Alice's transaction to her has failed. When Bob searches for his public key, he can see that Alice's 0.5 bitcoin was sent to his public key. Bob's private key now acts as the only key that will unlock those 0.5 bitcoin units in the network. Only the current owner of a particular amount of bitcoin can send it to someone else using their private key. The transparent public keys used in bitcoin transactions keeps everyone aware of what is going on and ensures no double-spending, yet still maintains security for the e-currency and the individuals involved.

How Secure Are Bitcoin Keys?

A Bitcoin wallet is a type of computer software that is used to create and store cryptographic keys. The wallet software can randomly generate new public and private keys without connecting to the Bitcoin network or to the internet. There is no need to check for duplicate keys, as the probabilities of duplication are astronomically small.

The odds of Bitcoin key duplication are 1 in 115.8 quattuorvigintillion, which is a 78 digit number. To put this in perspective, there are up to 400 billion stars in the Milky Way Galaxy, which is a 12 digit number. According to astronomers, there are approximately 170 billion galaxies in the observable universe, each with a varying amount of stars of their own. If those 170 billion galaxies are multiplied by the number of stars in the Milky Way, there would be 68 sextillion stars, which is only a 23 digit number. To reach the 78 digit combination of Bitcoin keys, this equation would need to assume that a **multiverse** exists with parallel universes that have a similar number of stars to our own. There would have to be 1.703 septendecillion multiverses, which is a 55 digit number. If all of the stars were added up in every multiverse, there would be about 115.8 quattuorvigintillion stars, which finally equals the 78 digit number of bitcoin key combinations.

By the end of the first decade of Bitcoin's history, more than 22 million public keys maintained a bitcoin balance. That equates to only 0.0055 percent of all of the stars in the Milky Way Galaxy, let alone the observable universe, or hypothetical multiverses. Cracking one of these key combinations is not impossible, but a 1 in 115.8 quattuorvigintillion chance establishes a level of security that is difficult to ignore.

Digital Signatures

To spend his bitcoin, Bob must prove to everyone in the network that he is the true owner of the public key that received 0.5 bitcoin from Alice. To accomplish this, Bob must create a digital signature that everyone in the network is able to verify. Bob's original transaction with Alice was assigned a transaction number, known as a hash. Bob uses this hash along with his private key to cryptographically create a digital signature. This digital signature is also tied to Bob's public key. Everyone in the network can use Bob's public key to verify that his digital signature is authentic. In this way, the private key acts as the true password, and the digital signature is a validator that proves Bob possesses the password. Bob does not need to reveal his password to anyone in the network to prove his ownership of Alice's spent bitcoin.

In Nakamoto's whitepaper, he credits Adam Back for Bitcoin's hash function. Back is the inventor of hashcash, a proof-of-work system that is used to defend against spam in emails.

How Is a Hash Created for a Digital Signature?

A cryptographic hash is a complex math equation that can reduce any amount of text into a string of numbers and letters. In Bitcoin, a hashing function called SHA-256 converts data into a string of 64 characters. As an example, the following text would always hash into a specific string using SHA-256.

The quick brown fox jumps over the lazy dog
D7A8FBB307D7809469CA9ABCB0082E4F8D5651E46D3CDB762D02D0BF37C9E592 ←——— Hash

However, if one period is added to the end of the text, the entire cryptographic hash would change.

Added period
The quick brown fox jumps over the lazy dog.
EF537F25C895BFA782526529A9B63D97AA631564D5D789C2B765448C8635FB6C ←——— Hash

When a Bitcoin transaction is hashed, the amount of bitcoin units being sent, as well as the public keys of the sender and recipient, are reduced to 64 characters. Once this hash is created, no one can change the transaction details or the hash would also need to change. This concept creates a unique hash for every bitcoin transaction. To add an additional level of security, since every digital signature requires a hash of the transaction, each digital signature will be unique. This makes it impossible for someone to reuse someone's digital signature to forge a transaction. In such a situation, peers in the network would reject the transaction, as the digital signature would not match the transaction data.

The Blockchain

The ownership of bitcoin is passed along in a transaction chain, where a person's claim can only be verified by referencing previous transactions. If Bob wants to buy a computer from Carol that costs 0.2 bitcoin more than the 0.5 bitcoin he received from Alice, Bob would also have to reference bitcoin he had received in a previous transaction. Bob could use a 0.3 bitcoin transaction he had received one year ago, along with his 0.5 bitcoin from Alice, to come up with 0.8 bitcoin. Next, Bob has to create a transaction that uses the entire 0.8 bitcoin, as the network requires that each transaction is used up completely. Bob would use his private key to create a digital signature that references both the 0.3 and the 0.5 bitcoin transactions. Eventually, Bob's 0.8 bitcoin transaction would be validated by peers in the Bitcoin network.

Carol would receive 0.7 bitcoin from Bob, and 0.1 bitcoin, minus a small transaction fee, would be returned to Bob. Carol's ownership of 0.7 bitcoin, and Bob's nearly 0.1 bitcoin would now reside in the most current Bitcoin block.

With the Bitcoin blockchain, Satoshi Nakamoto created a system of decentralized trust. Peers in the network trust that regardless of a person's intent to steal funds, individual transactions that were successfully added to a block could be trusted. However, Nakamoto also needed to implement a mechanism for ensuring that someone could not go back to a previous block in the blockchain and change a transaction. To accomplish this, Nakamoto found a way to make the blockchain **immutable** using a concept known as proof-of-work.

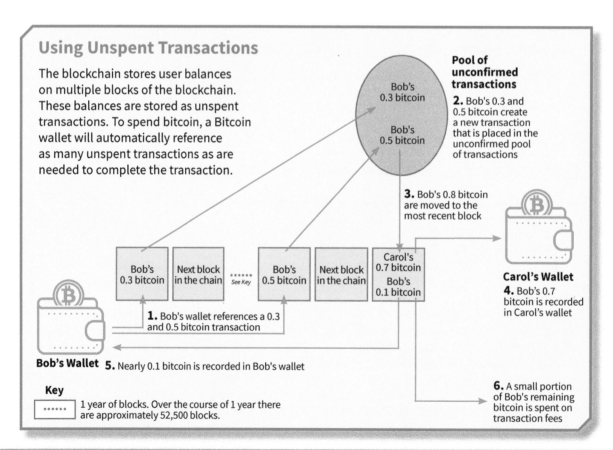

Using Unspent Transactions

The blockchain stores user balances on multiple blocks of the blockchain. These balances are stored as unspent transactions. To spend bitcoin, a Bitcoin wallet will automatically reference as many unspent transactions as are needed to complete the transaction.

Bob's 0.3 bitcoin

Bob's 0.5 bitcoin

Pool of unconfirmed transactions

2. Bob's 0.3 and 0.5 bitcoin create a new transaction that is placed in the unconfirmed pool of transactions

3. Bob's 0.8 bitcoin are moved to the most recent block

| Bob's 0.3 bitcoin | Next block in the chain | ...... See Key | Bob's 0.5 bitcoin | Next block in the chain | Carol's 0.7 bitcoin
Bob's 0.1 bitcoin |

Carol's Wallet
4. Bob's 0.7 bitcoin is recorded in Carol's wallet

1. Bob's wallet references a 0.3 and 0.5 bitcoin transaction

Bob's Wallet **5.** Nearly 0.1 bitcoin is recorded in Bob's wallet

6. A small portion of Bob's remaining bitcoin is spent on transaction fees

Key

...... 1 year of blocks. Over the course of 1 year there are approximately 52,500 blocks.

In Bitcoin's Genesis Block, Satoshi Nakamoto included the text "*The Times* 03/Jan/2009 Chancellor on brink of second bailout for banks." This reference highlighted the practice of governments giving banks billions of dollars to save them from financial collapse.

Proof-of-Work

On January 3, 2009, Satoshi Nakamoto activated Bitcoin software on his computer that created the first Bitcoin block. This block, known as the Genesis Block, was created through a concept known as proof-of-work. Nakamoto's computer was required to solve a complex math problem in order to create the first Bitcoin block. To solve the math problem, the computer needed to expend a certain amount of electricity. Expended electricity, along with the answer to a math problem, is what makes up the Bitcoin software's definition of proof-of-work.

Bitcoin's proof-of-work relies on people called miners that compete to solve each Bitcoin block. They compete for an amount of bitcoin that is awarded to the person whose computer solves that particular block's math problem. This reward is called a coinbase, and it is the only way that units of bitcoin are created. To fully understand why proof-of-work is important, it is valuable to see an example of what this math problem looks like, how difficult is it to solve, and why miners around the world let their computers try to solve it.

Bitcoin miners will receive coinbase rewards until 21 million bitcoins have been created.

Mining Difficulty

To compete for coinbase awards, miners begin by creating a hash of all transactions inside each block. This works similarly to creating a hash to represent a single Bitcoin transaction. However, when creating a hash for a Bitcoin block, Nakamoto added a level of difficulty. Miners would need to add a string of numbers, called a **nonce**, to the end of each block. The right combination of numbers in the nonce creates a certain amount of zeros at the beginning of the hash. Miners search for this nonce value by making multiple rapid-guesses, until their hash value has enough leading zeroes. If the text "Hello, world!" represents a Bitcoin transaction block, it would need a nonce value of 4250 to create four zeroes at the start of its hash.

There is no math equation that would make it easier for a miner to calculate a nonce value. If Alice becomes a Bitcoin miner, and she started with a nonce value of 1, she would need to make 4,250 guesses before coming up with a nonce that would solve the 4-zero proof-of-work example above.

Using Nonce Values

Hello, world!4250 ← Nonce

0000C3AF42FC31103F1FDC0151FA747FF87349A4714DF7CC52EA464E12DCD4E9 ← Hash

Without the nonce value of 4250, the hash would have no leading zeros.

Hello, world!

315F5BDB76D078C43B8AC0064E4A0164612B1FCE77C869345BFC94C75894EDD3 ← Hash

See page 44 for instructions on how to duplicate the above hashes, or to create your own hash.

Difficulty Levels

In Bitcoin's early days, the network required that eight zeroes be added to the beginning of a hash. As time passed, the Bitcoin network automatically adjusted the difficulty level by adding or removing zeros from the requirement. The difficulty level fluctuates to ensure that a Bitcoin block is solved every 10 minutes on average. The difficulty level changes to keep pace with faster computing power, and the inconsistency of miners who are participating in the network. About a decade after Bitcoin first started, the network reached a difficulty level of 18 zeros at the start of a hash.

Mining a Double-Spend

Once a Bitcoin block is assigned a hash, the next block includes this hash number as part of its data. This creates a chain between blocks, with hash numbers acting as links in the chain. This is where the term blockchain originates. Through mining, Alice could make another attempt at double-spending by sending the same bitcoin units to Bob and Carol. If Alice tried to go back five blocks and replace her transaction to Bob with her transaction to Carol, the hash of that block would change. This would break the chain, as the immediate block ahead of Alice's altered block would no longer include the correct hash number.

Other miners would never accept Alice's broken chain, as the Bitcoin network always follows the longest valid chain. However, what if Alice decided to only go back one block? Alice would wait for it to be mined by the network so that Bob would receive confirmation that he received Alice's bitcoin. Then, Alice would need to re-mine the entire block, as well as the next block in the blockchain, before the next block is solved by other miners. In this way, Alice would possess the longest chain, causing all other miners to accept her chain as the main valid chain. However, with the Bitcoin network's built in difficulty levels, this would be nearly impossible for Alice to accomplish.

Bitcoin mining equipment can calculate 12 trillion nonces, or hashes, per second. In contrast, most desktop computers achieve only 4 million hashes per second.

Electricity Costs

Mining difficulty levels force mining hardware to expend electricity in order to find nonce values quickly. If Alice purchased a consumer grade bitcoin miner, such as the Antminer S9, the device would use roughly 1 million **joules** of energy in 10 minutes. However, the entire Bitcoin network expends about 1.5 trillion joules in 10 minutes. This means that the network is expending 1.5 million times more joules than Alice, giving her a 1 in 1.5 million chance of mining a block faster than the network.

If Alice was extremely lucky, and re-mined Bob's block in under 10 minutes, she would need to immediately start work on mining the next block in the chain. However, while Alice was re-mining the previous block, other miners in the network were hard at work solving the next block in the main chain. The Bitcoin network's combined processing power of 1.5 trillion joules

In 2021, the Bitcoin network consumed more than 121 terawatt-hours (TWh) of electricity a year. This is more electricity than the country of Argentina uses each year.

makes it astronomically unlikely that Alice's 1 million joules could ever mine the next block before another miner. In this case, Bob can be reasonably confident that his transaction is secure on the blockchain.

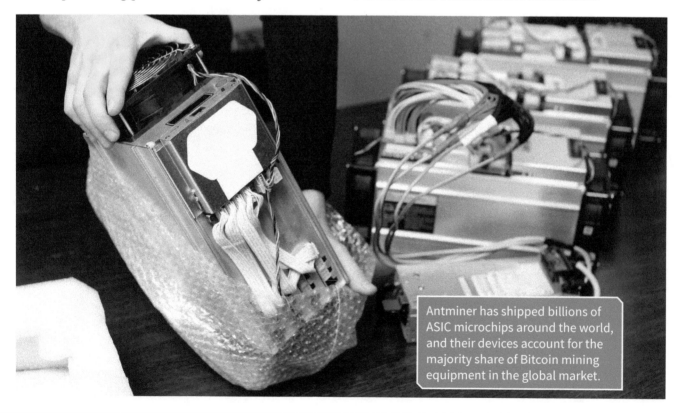

Antminer has shipped billions of ASIC microchips around the world, and their devices account for the majority share of Bitcoin mining equipment in the global market.

Mounting a Network Attack

What if Alice owned several data centers, and controlled 10 percent of the Bitcoin network's computing power? She would have a 10 percent chance of mining her first block faster than the network, and only a 5 percent chance of mining the second block. If Bob is worried about the possibility of this type of a double-spend from Alice, he could simply wait for 6 blocks to be added to the blockchain. Alice would have a 0.024 percent chance of mining these six blocks in a row. In fact, mining six blocks in a row last occurred on January 6, 2014, by a **mining pool** named GHash.

For Bob to be extremely confident that his bitcoin from Alice are secure, he should wait for at least six blocks to be added to the blockchain after his block. This is called waiting for six confirmations, and is a common practice among users of Bitcoin. As more blocks get added to Bob's chain, his transaction becomes immutable, as the energy required to erase Bob's transaction and create a longer chain becomes virtually impossible.

To cheat the network, malicious miners would have to know that they are about to get lucky, and solve several blocks in a row. Since the math used to solve a block is random, mining blocks in a row is impossible to predict. By requiring difficult math problems to be solved with each block, attackers like Alice are unlikely to win a **computational** race against the entire Bitcoin network.

The Bitcoin network adjusts mining difficulty levels every **2016 blocks**, which takes **2 weeks** to complete with 10 minute block averages.

Bitcoin's hash rate increases by an average of **16%** every **2 weeks**.

The Antminer S19 Pro uses **3,250 watts** of power.

Maintaining a 51% Attack

A 51 percent attack is a theoretical scenario where a miner has 51 percent of the Bitcoin network's computing power. In this scenario, a miner could prevent new transactions, and double-spend their own transactions. By expending more joules than the rest of the network, this miner has a higher probability of winning more blocks than anyone else. If Alice wanted to mount a 51 percent attack, she could spend all of her bitcoin over the course of three Bitcoin blocks. During this time, Alice would be mining her own private chain that does not include her spent transactions.

Since Alice has more computing power than the rest of the network, her private chain will eventually become longer than the main chain. When this happens, Alice would announce her chain to the rest of the network. Since Alice's chain is the longest chain, the network will automatically accept her chain as the valid chain, and Alice's spent transactions will be erased from the blockchain.

In theory, a 51 percent attack is the only way to guarantee that someone could double-spend a transaction. However, in practicality it would require dedicated power plants, and cost more than 1 billion dollars in computational power and mining equipment to execute such a heist, making it unlikely that a 51 percent attack would occur.

Bitcoin Software

When Bitcoin's software was first created by Satoshi Nakamoto it was simply called "Bitcoin" or "Satoshi Client." After many modifications and improvements the software evolved into what is now known as "Bitcoin Core." As of 2021, more than 800 software developers have contributed to Bitcoin Core.

In the early days, Satoshi Nakamoto and several collaborators would fix frequent bugs in the software. Early Bitcoin developers included Hal Finney, Martti "Sirius" Malmi, and Gavin Andresen. The second version of Bitcoin's software was released nearly twelve months after Bitcoin's inception on January 3, 2009. It included **Linux** compatablility and made use of multi-core processors for mining. On April 23, 2011, Satoshi Nakamoto left the Bitcoin community, telling his successor Gavin Andresen, that he has moved on to other things.

Today, tens of thousands of people around the world run the Bitcoin Core software. These people are called **nodes**. Nodes maintain a complete record of every transaction on the blockchain from the

Gavin Andresen graduated from Princeton with a computer science degree in 1998, developing 3D graphics and virtual reality modeling. He began working alongside Satoshi Nakamoto in December 2010.

Genesis Block to the present. While many run the lastest version of Bitcoin Core, every node in the network runs independent versions of the software. A significant number of nodes continue to run older versions of Bitcoin Core to validate blocks. In this way, trivial changes to Bitcoin Core can be accepted or rejected by nodes, and the software will continue to function.

Gavin Andresen's Bitcoin Faucet

In 2010, Bitcoin Core developer, Gavin Andresen created a website to give away bitcoin for free. All users had to do was complete a captcha, enter their Bitcoin Address, and they would receive 5 bitcoins. Satoshi Nakamoto wrote that this was an "excellent choice of a first project... I had planned to do this exact thing if someone else didn't do it..." When the site closed in 2012, more than 19,700 bitcoins were distributed, helping the currency gain traction among internet users.

In fact, several Bitcoin Core developers, including Gavin Andresen, have encouraged developers to expand the network with their own implementations of Bitcoin software. This means that software changes can be made by nodes, independed of Bitcoin Core, and they can still access the Bitcoin network. If any software changes go against Bitcoin's consensus rules, such as the predictable rate at which new bitcoins are created, those nodes will fall our of sync and lose access to the network.

Soft Forks

A soft fork occurs when new rules are added or tightened in the Bitcoin protocol. A famous example of a soft fork occured when developer Pieter Wuille proposed a change in the way that transaction data was stored. He proposed that moving digital signatures attached to transactions to a sidechain would make the network more secure. This was called Segregated Witness (SegWit) and it was implemented in 2017. Nodes that upgraded to the SegWit protocol would see the Bitcoin blockchain and the SegWit sidechain running parallel to each other.

SegWit had the added benefit of freeing up space within each Bitcoin block. With blocks having a size limit of 1 megabyte (MB), digital signatures comprised about 65 percent of each block. The removal of digital signatures allowed for more transactions to be included in each block, making the whole network faster. The creation of a sidechain also made it possible for the implementation of the Lightning Network, a micropayment channel with lower transaction fees (see page 32).

SegWit is a soft fork because it was backward compatible. This means that nodes who did not upgrade to the SegWit protocol could still interact with upgraded nodes and participate in the network. After one year, more than 30 percent of nodes implemented the SegWit protocol. If the SegWit protocal was not backwards compatible, it would be called a **hard fork**.

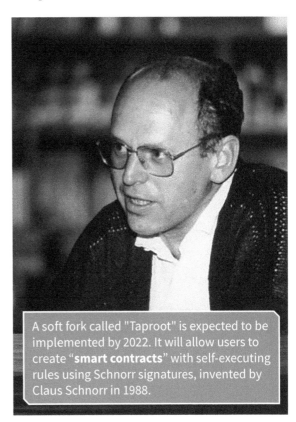

A soft fork called "Taproot" is expected to be implemented by 2022. It will allow users to create "**smart contracts**" with self-executing rules using Schnorr signatures, invented by Claus Schnorr in 1988.

Hard Forks

Hard forks eliminate or loosen existing rules. They are not backward compatible. This means that nodes who do not upgrade to new software protocols cannot interact with upgraded nodes. Hard forks can result in two networks; one managed by nodes with a brand-new set of rules, and one maintained by nodes with the original set of rules. The most famous example of a hard fork occured on August 1, 2017 with the creation of Bitcoin Cash.

When SegWit was first proposed, there was a fundamental disagreement on whether it was the best approach. Some argued fervently that SegWit's ability to create a separate payment channel off-chain was contrary to the foundations in which Bitcoin was built. Craig Wright, a Satoshi Nakamoto identity-claimant, argued that an off-chain payment system would be "an alteration of the system to remove logs long-term," effectively making Bitcoin anonymous. Some argued that off-chain transactions created a trusted system, which would defy one of Bitcoin's basic principles on third parties being untrustworthy.

By 2021, Bitcoin had more than 10,000 nodes running the network. That was about 90 percent more network nodes than Bitcoin Cash.

With these disagreements, SegWit detractors proposed an alternate solution to increase the number of transactions processed per block. They decided to change Bitcoin's 1 MB block size to 8 MB. To participate in a network with larger block sizes, nodes would need to have the ability to download more data. Nodes with older computers, or slower internet speeds would run the risk of not receiving blocks within 10 minute intervals. This would make it difficult for individuals to operate as nodes from their homes, giving an advantage to private companies with larger financial resources.

Some developers began work on software protocols that would increase block sizes to 8 MB. Because there was not universal consensus about this adoption, it resulted in the split of the blockchain into a new branch. The nodes that implemented the 8 MB block size change re-branded their blockchain as Bitcoin Cash, while the nodes that kept the 1 MB block size retained the original name of Bitcoin.

Quote from Satoshi Nakamoto

"The nature of Bitcoin is such that once version 0.1 was released, the core design was set in stone for the rest of its lifetime... I don't believe a second, compatible implementation of Bitcoin will ever be a good idea. So much of the design depends on all nodes getting exactly identical results in lockstep that a second implementation would be a menace to the network."

June 17, 2010

The Bitcoin Cash software implementation was a hard fork that resulted in the creation of a new blockchain branch because the software changes were not backwards compatible. While any block with a block size of 1 MB could be considered valid by both Bitcoin nodes and Bitcoin Cash nodes, only Bitcoin Cash nodes could validate blocks between 1 and 8 MB. This backwards incompatibility is the direct result of eliminating existing protocol rules.

The Bitcoin Cash hard fork occured at block number 478559. Anyone who owned units of bitcoin before this block would be granted the same amount of Bitcoin Cash units. This effectively created two currencies. After block 478558, nodes on the Bitcoin network and Bitcoin Cash network only processed their own chain, avoiding any issues with double spending. On November 15, 2020, Bitcoin Cash experienced it's own hard fork. The Bitcoin Cash camp supported by entrepreneur Roger Ver and Bitmain decided

The Bitcoin network uses about 99 percent more energy than Bitcoin Cash. This makes the Bitcoin Cash network 99 percent more susceptible to a 51 percent attack.

to increase the block size to 32 MB. Craig Wright led a second camp called Bitcoin Satoshi Vision (Bitcoin SV) that supported a block size limit of 128 MB. Bitcoin SV hard forked from Bitcoin Cash at block 620538 forming its own branch.

The Bitcoin Cash and Bitcoin SV Hard Forks

In the month leading to the Bitcoin Cash hard fork, many Bitcoin blocks frequently reached a 0.99 MB block size. On the day of the hard fork, transactions slowed down near block 478559 as network users curiously watched the event unfold. While only minutes passed before Bitcoin block 478559 was mined, nearly 5 hours went by before Block 478559 was mined in the Bitcoin Cash network.

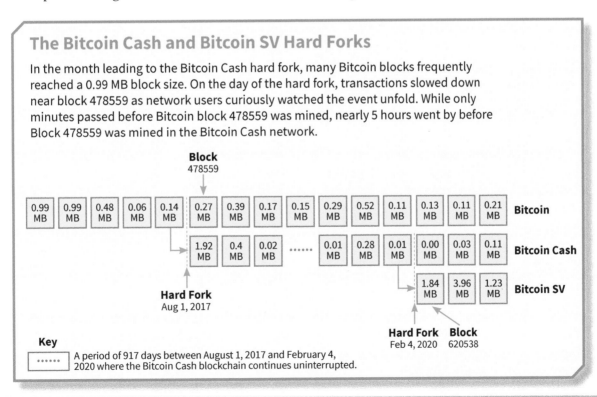

Block 478559

| 0.99 MB | 0.99 MB | 0.48 MB | 0.06 MB | 0.14 MB | 0.27 MB | 0.39 MB | 0.17 MB | 0.15 MB | 0.29 MB | 0.52 MB | 0.11 MB | 0.13 MB | 0.11 MB | 0.21 MB | **Bitcoin** |

| 1.92 MB | 0.4 MB | 0.02 MB | ...... | 0.01 MB | 0.28 MB | 0.01 MB | 0.00 MB | 0.03 MB | 0.11 MB | **Bitcoin Cash** |

| 1.84 MB | 3.96 MB | 1.23 MB | **Bitcoin SV** |

Hard Fork
Aug 1, 2017

Hard Fork **Block**
Feb 4, 2020 620538

Key

...... A period of 917 days between August 1, 2017 and February 4, 2020 where the Bitcoin Cash blockchain continues uninterrupted.

Experts estimate that each of the approximately 2.3 million blocks of the Great Pyramid of Giza were stacked in place every 2.5 minutes during daylight. In contrast, Bitcoin blocks are continuously added to the blockchain, regardless of the time of day.

The Future of Bitcoin

Examples of Bitcoin's proof-of-work mechanism can be seen in the physical world. Proof-of-work was used in the making of the Great Pyramid of Giza in the 26th century BC. The 451 foot (138 meter) monument is a declaration to every civilization that arose after the Egyptians. The structure is proof that the Egyptians had abundant resources to feed about 20,000 people to focus their energy on construction. The endeavour would also require decades of time in dedication to the work of adding an average block size of 2.6 tons (2.36 metric tons) on top of another.

The Great Pyramid of Giza stands today as a testament to the proof-of-work of the Egyptian civilization. In later years, proof-of-work was also used to create other structures around the world, including the Colosseum in Rome, the Taj Mahal in India, and the Great Wall of China.

Up until the 21st century, humanity has only seen examples of proof-of-work in physical environments. Here, people in one geographic area worked together in a common cause. In 2009, Satoshi Nakamoto laid the building blocks for the first digital monument of proof-of-work. Since then, participants have been working on a global scale, as geographic locations no longer matter. However, unlike physical examples of proof-of-work, Bitcoin is becoming a record of unchangeable history. Ancient monuments can be destroyed in an instant with the drop of an atom bomb, while established history on the blockchain cannot be modified by any sudden attack.

Most large Bitcoin mining centers are located in areas where there is an availability of surplus energy at a reduced rate. Bitcoin mining near hydroelectric plants help to normalize energy markets by consuming surplus energy that would otherwise go to waste.

Energy As Security

Each block on the blockchain took a certain amount of joules to build. As time passes, new blocks take more-and-more energy to build. Storing bitcoin on a block of the blockchain is equivalent to placing valuables in a safe, and every 10 minutes, that safe is placed into another locked safe. With proof-of-work, expended energy creates a level of increased security that is not present in any financial system on Earth.

The traditional banking system has no system in place to guarantee the security of transactions. There is no significant energy cost, measured in joules, for a bank to revoke a transaction that was sent one week earlier. A court order can force a bank to reverse bank transactions. Therefore, an individual's transaction in the banking system is not secure. Transaction history on the Bitcoin blockchain is written by the expenditure of joules, and there is no easy way to erase that history.

Psyche is an asteroid in Earth's solar system. Astronomers believe that the precious metals contained in Psyche are worth $10,000 Quadrillion.

Chargebacks

The security of the Bitcoin network would also help merchants who struggle with transaction reversals called chargebacks. This occurs when customers bypass merchants, and go directly to their bank to request a debit or credit card refund. About 86 percent of all chargebacks are cases of **friendly fraud**. When this happens, merchants get stuck with transaction and bank fees that amount to about $25 billion each year. Globally, chargebacks cost merchants approximately 0.47 percent of their total yearly revenue. The blockchain's energy cost does not allow friendly fraud to take place, as transaction reversals are not possible. This makes customers deal directly with merchants for refunds. In the case of merchant fraud, local authorities would be the main recourse for consumers.

In spite of Bitcoin's advantages over debit and credit cards, people may still argue that using traditional financial systems such as gold and paper currencies are the most secure. However, this may not be true. Today, new frontiers mean a greater likelihood that a flood of commodities, like the Spanish silver boom of the 16th century, will throw markets off balance. Space mining companies Deep Space Industries and Planetary Resources are developing ways to mine asteroids that approach Earth. Astronomers predict that one such asteroid could hold more gold than all of the gold mined in Earth's history. Such a find would cause the value of gold to plummet, reducing the buying power of the commodity.

Merchants lose about **$15 billion** each year in online credit card fraud.

Instead of contacting merchants, about **81%** of customers admit to filing chargebacks out of convenience.

Approximately 40% of consumers who commit friendly fraud, do it again within **60 days.**

Printing Paper Currencies

The value of paper currencies continues to diminish every year as governments print more and more money. This causes the global price of goods to rise by about 3.5 percent each year, while income levels rise on average by 1 percent. This discrepancy is in effect, an added tax. It is less of a struggle for governments to print an endless supply of money than it is to convince the public that raising income or sales taxes are a good idea. Sometimes, governments are impelled to act quickly in times of desperation. On March 27, 2020, the United States Congress passed a $2.2 trillion stimulus bill to mitigate the economic fallout of the COVID-19 pandemic.

Future Developments

Unlike traditional currencies, bitcoin has a finite supply, as only 21 million digital coins can ever be created. In fact, by the year 2140, the last bitcoin will be mined. At that point, miners will continue mining operations for rewards in transaction fees. Bitcoin is still in its infancy. However developments are being made to improve the network.

To allow more people to use bitcoin, the amount of transactions that can be included in one block has been adjusted three times. However, developers are cautious on increasing transaction capacity as it causes miners to expend more energy. As electricity costs rise, miners are turning to renewable energy sources. This is helping to fund hydroelectric, wind, and solar farms.

The energy expended in the Bitcoin network is an investment in the security of a financial network that no individual, corporation, bank, or government can control. This energy expenditure is the cost of true monetary freedom. Bitcoin's proof-of-work consensus algorithm introduces a tamper-proof form of permanent digital history. If Bitcoin survives for 1,000 years, there will be 52.5 million blocks stacked on top of each other. It will become a demonstration of our generation's ability to create an immutable history. As there are 7 wonders in the physical world, Bitcoin is perhaps the first example of a wonder in the digital world.

West Texas produces 30% of all wind power in the United States, making electricity costs in the state cheaper than most places on Earth. Because of this, west Texas is home to some of the largest Bitcoin mining companies in the world.

The Lightning Network

The Lightning Network is a peer-to-peer system for making payments outside of the Bitcoin network. The Lightning Network is a new layer in Bitcoin's architecture that aims to allow small Bitcoin transactions to take place outside of the regular blockchain. This is projected to increase the speed of day-to-day transactions and lower the network's energy consumption significantly.

To access the Lightning Network, a Bitcoin user opens up a payment channel on the Bitcoin network with a node on the Lightning Network. A payment channel essentially locks up a certain amount of bitcoin until either the Bitcoin user or the node decides to close the channel. A simple example follows the interaction of two parties. If Alice visits Disneyland, she can open a payment channel for 0.05 bitcoin with a Disney node on the Lightning Network to make several small transactions inside the park. When Alice leaves Disneyland she can close her payment channel on the bitcoin network, settling all of her Disneyland purchases in one transaction on the blockchain.

Transaction fees on the Lightning Network can be less than 0.00000001 bitcoin (1 Satoshi). Conversely, on the bitcoin network, 1 Satoshi is the smallest unit, and is not divisible.

A complex example includes all participants on the Lightning Network. Alice does not need to close her payment channel with Disneyland if she wants to make another off-chain purchase for coffee. Instead, Alice can pay for her coffee through the Disney node. The Disney node would pass on Alice's transaction to someone who has a payment channel set up with the Disney node and the coffee shop's node. If Bob was the intermediary, then he would act as the node between Disneyland and the coffee shop.

The advantages of using the Lightning Network includes increased privacy, faster transactions, and lower fees. Firstly, Bob does not see Alice's payment to the coffee shop, he only sees the transaction sent to him from the Disney node, and the transaction he sends to the coffee shop. This factor relies on the Lighting Network being decentralized, whereby anyone can be a node. Secondly, the transaction can occur in a split-second instead of taking approximately 10 minutes on the Bitcoin network. Also, the Bitcoin network can handle about 3 to 7 transactions per second as each Bitcoin block can only store a maximum of 1 megabytes of data. The Lighting Network has no block-size constraints, and can process millions of transactions per second. Thirdly, since the Lightning Network does not need to expend energy to solve a proof-of-work, transaction fees are projected to be much lower than the Bitcoin network.

Without a proof-of-work mechanism, the Lighting Network does have a drawback. The Lightning Network is unable to secure transactions under layers of expended energy making the storage of funds less secure than the Bitcoin network. This means that the Lightning Network will likely be

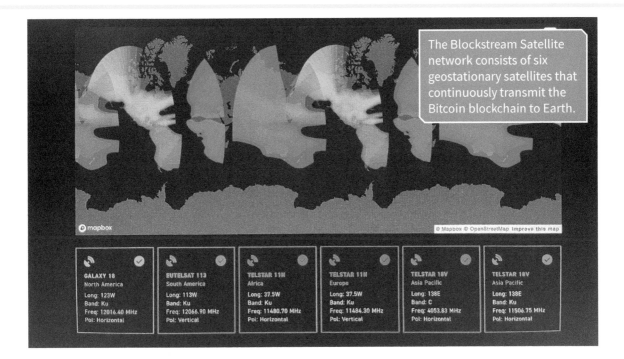

The Blockstream Satellite network consists of six geostationary satellites that continuously transmit the Bitcoin blockchain to Earth.

GALAXY 18	EUTELSAT 113	TELSTAR 11N	TELSTAR 11N	TELSTAR 18V	TELSTAR 18V
North America	South America	Africa	Europe	Asia Pacific	Asia Pacific
Long: 123W	Long: 113W	Long: 37.5W	Long: 37.5W	Long: 138E	Long: 138E
Band: Ku	Band: Ku	Band: Ku	Band: Ku	Band: C	Band: Ku
Freq: 12016.40 MHz	Freq: 12066.90 MHz	Freq: 11480.70 MHz	Freq: 11484.30 MHz	Freq: 4053.83 MHz	Freq: 11506.75 MHz
Pol: Horizontal	Pol: Vertical	Pol: Horizontal	Pol: Vertical	Pol: Horizontal	Pol: Horizontal

used for smaller day-to-day purchases. Acquiring items such as computers and vehicles are more likely to be settled on the Bitcoin network for increased security. Another worry among some in the Bitcoin community is that government regulation could force businesses to use a government approved Lightning Network. In this scenario, nodes could be run by financial institutions that charge high fees and track transactions, making the network no different than today's centralized monetary system. Despite these concerns, for the first time in Bitcoin's history, the speed of the Lighting Network would allow for worldwide mass-adoption of Bitcoin.

The Bitcoin Satellite Network

Blockstream is a blockchain technology company co-founded by Adam Back in 2014. The company provides a wide range of products, including hardware wallets and their own implementation of the Lightning Network protocol. They also maintain a satellite network that broadcasts the Bitcoin blockchain around the world.

To run the network, Blockstream ground stations across the globe participate in the Bitcoin network. They transmit signals to each other to make sure they are in sync, and transmit blocks to satellites in **geosynchronous** oribit. Orbiting at an altitude of 22,236 miles (35,786 km), Blockstream satellites broadcast the signal across much of Earth's surface. Anyone with a satellite antenna can receive these Bitcoin blocks, view transactions, and verify that their network connection is accurate.

The Blockstream satellite network encircles the globe, providing a secondary layer of redundancy to the Bitcoin blockchain. This protects against network interruptions and provides access to the Bitcoin network to those who live in areas with unreliable internet connections. The satellite network also bypasses political sensorship in areas where internet connections are censored by governments. In the process of eliminating cost barriers, more people around the world can use Bitcoin and participate in the Bitcoin network.

Bitcoin Safety

Bitcoin's early history has been plagued with frequent media stories involving lost or stolen funds. Sometimes, these stories involved unregulated exchanges. However, even the most reputable cryptocurrency exchange platforms have experienced sophisticated attacks. A unifying theme of these attacks are centralized servers which hackers are able to penetrate.

Hacks

One of the earliest, and perhaps the most well-known hack in Bitcoin history, was the attack on the cryptocurrency exchange, Mt. Gox. The company went bankrupt in 2014 after announcing that hackers had stolen 840,000 bitcoins which were valued at $460 million at the time. Shortly after the hack, Mt. Gox found 200,000 bitcoins on an old-format digital wallet. Following a lengthy legal battle, Mt. Gox customers are expected to receive 23 percent of their original bitcoin holdings after an agreement was reached with bankruptcy trustees in 2021.

After the Mt. Gox incident, high profile hacks continued to plague cryptocurrency exchanges every year. Despite this reality, many Bitcoin users resigned themselves to the use of centralized exchanges in the ecosystem, leaving their funds on exchanges for months at a time. These users are able to protect their accounts with **two-factor authentication**, but centralized exchanges hold the private keys that are able to access the actual bitcoin on the blockchain. When bitcoin is traded on a centralized exchange, the internal ledger of the centralized exchange keeps track of each user's bitcoin balance, but the transaction is not recorded on the blockchain. Hardened

More than $2 billion has been hacked from cryptocurrency exchanges between 2011 and 2021.

Bitcoin users treat exchanges as a hot potato, quickly executing trades and immediately withdrawing funds. Once funds are withdrawn from an exchange, the Bitcoin transaction is recorded on the blockchain, and access to that bitcoin is only accessible with a private key. Usually, bitcoin is withdrawn to a hot or cold wallet.

Wallets

A hot wallet can be a software application that is downloaded from the internet. The hot wallet resides on a users computer, and the private keys are contained within the application. While safer than storing bitcoin on an exchange, a hot wallet is still vulnerable to hackers, as hackers could gain access to a computer and drain the wallet by accessing the software application.

Quote from Satoshi Nakamoto

"Sigh... why delete a wallet instead of moving it aside and keeping the old copy just in case? You should never delete a wallet."

October 3, 2010

Storage devices, such as a USB drive, can be used to store bitcoin keys. There are several types of hardware wallets with greater security than USB devices. Many of these hardware wallets, often referred to as a cold wallet, offer complete isolation between the private key stored on the device and a user's computer. Good hardware wallets are resiliant from online hackers.

When offline, hardware wallets are deemed to be in cold storage. This is considered to be the safest way to store Bitcoin keys. Sometimes Bitcoin public and private keys are printed on paper. This is called a paper wallet. A **QR code** is usually printed with the wallet so that users can quickly scan the keys to add them to a software wallet. Paper wallets should be treated as cash, duplicated, and placed in a safe place. If anyone were to find this paper wallet, they would be able to transfer all of its bitcoin to their own wallet.

Decentralized Exchanges

Many early Bitcoin users who found pride in their involvement in building a decentralized currency, found themselves trapped with an unhealthy reliance on centralized servers to exchange value. Decentralized exchanges

Hardware Wallet Safety

Hardware wallets usually create Bitcoin keys out of 24 seed words. This a called a **mnemonic phrase**. During set-up, a hardware wallet will prompt users to write these words on paper. The mnemonic phrase should be kept in a safe place. If a hardware wallet is lost or damaged, the mnemonic phrase is the only way to restore the wallet on a new device. Sometimes, scammers will attempt **phishing** attacks to get users to divulge mnemonic phrases. Hardware wallet manufacturers will never request mnemonic phrases. Never reveal your seed words to anyone.

allow users to retain complete control over their private keys, and they must use those keys to verify each transaction. Amidst the headline grabbing stories of bitoin hacks, it is possible to have a safe experience by keeping private keys in a safe place.

Bitcoin Keys

Create Bitcoin keys using a website such as https://www.bitaddress.org. Shake your mouse to help generate random numbers for your keys. Print or save these keys in a safe place. Your public address can be shared with other people. This is your Bitcoin address, and is used by other people to send you bitcoin. Never share your private key with anyone. If someone has your private key, they can steal your bitcoin. You can unlock your funds at any time using your private key. Many security experts recommend disconnecting from the internet when generating private keys.

15VJosWYq6NsCqtavBz3UDuBSMk1bC3fdXg ←——— Bitcoin Address
L3vweJcJfoNv4SWvWp7doCkyd3tHnXzLmTf5wAxTL5qknp8JKAMw ←——— Private Key

A Bitcoin address is a hash (see page 17) of a public key. Bitcoin addresses are between 26-35 characters and usually begin with a 1, 3, or bc1. A Bitcoin private key is a large 256-bit number. *Do not send any bitcoin to the above Bitcoin address. Anyone reading this book can take those funds because they have access to the private key.*

Satoshi in the Media

Satoshi Nakamoto is the alias of the creator or creators of the Bitcoin software. The name first appeared online in conjunction with the Bitcoin whitepaper on October 31, 2008. The creator of Bitcoin may have wanted to remain anonymous for several reasons. To begin with, people in positions of power can cause price movements. In financial markets, a comment from a CEO can cause the price of their company to rise or fall. Also, nations can see the value of their currency drop if the words of central bank directors are taken out of context.

Nakamoto may have also been concerned about the legal repercussions of revealing his identity. In 2007, a gold-backed digital currency named e-gold was shut down by the U.S. government for failure to stop illegal transactions. Later, the creators of e-gold were sentenced to 3 years probation. Despite Nakamoto's reasons for remaining anonymous, media outlets have tried to discover his identity. The following people have been suspected by media outlets of being Satoshi Nakamoto.

Hal Finney

Hal Finney was a computer scientist and cryptographer who was involved in several digital currencies before Bitcoin. He is notable for pioneering key-signing for early PGP code. He also developed the first proof-of-work-based digital cash system called Reusable Proofs of Work (RPOW). On January 12, 2009, Finney was the first person to receive a Bitcoin transaction when Nakamoto sent him 10 bitcoins to test the system. He was also the first person, other than Nakamoto, to express optimism online about Bitcoin.

Throughout Bitcoin's early stages, Finney corresponded with Nakamoto, sending him bug reports and suggestions to fix the code. In later years, Finney wrote an improvement to Bitcoin's **elliptic-curve** cryptography that sped up transactions by about 20 percent. In March 2014, *Forbes* investigated Finney's involvement in Bitcoin. A journalist read

Creating Bitcoin: A Team of Experts, or a Lone Genius?

In 2008, security expert Dan Kaminsky discovered a weakness in the internet that would have allowed a skilled coder to take over any website, or even to shut down the internet itself. He contacted the Department of Homeland Security and helped them fix the vulnerability. In 2011, Kaminsky spent weeks trying to hack the Bitcoin protocol. Each time Kaminsky identified an attack vector, his bugs were rejected by the software. Kaminsky noted that Bitcoin's creator had a deep understanding of the C++ programming language, cryptography, economics, and peer-to-peer networking. He concluded that Bitcoin was either created by a team of people, or a lone genius.

In 1989, Nick Szabo graduated from the University of Washington with a degree in computer science. He also holds a law degree from George Washington University Law School.

In May 2015, the *New York Times* pegged Szabo as Bitcoin's creator, which he categorically denied. Today, Szabo is a well-respected member of the Bitcoin community. He is a strong supporter of developing the Lightning Network and other second-layer solutions to help Bitcoin meet increasing user demand. Interestingly, Sazbo corresponded extensively with Hal Finney about cryptographic payment schemes, they were both members of the cypherpunks mailing list, and members of an online message board that specialized in discussions on life-extension.

Craig Wright

Craig Wright is an Australian computer scientist and businessman. Wright holds six Master's degrees as well as a PHD in Philosophy. In December 2015, an article by *Wired* magazine claimed that Wright was the inventor of Bitcoin. Hours later, Australian police raided Wright's home and office. On May 2, 2016, Wright publicly announced that he and Dave Kleiman, an American computer forensics expert, were the creators of Bitcoin. Wright provided evidence in the form of a cryptographic signature tied to Bitcoin that was believed to have been mined by Satoshi Nakamoto. Wright's evidence has been controversial in the Bitcoin community, with widely divergent opinions.

On November 15, 2018, Craig Wright created Bitcoin SV, short for "Bitcoin Satoshi's Vision." The goal of the currency was to allow more transactions in each block and reduce transaction costs. In response, many prominent cryptocurrency figures called Wright a fraud. In May 2019, Wright served legal notices to his accusers, including Vitalic Buterin, the founder of Etherium, and Roger Ver, an early Bitcoin entrepreneur. In response, some major cryptocurrency exchanges delisted Bitcoin SV from their platforms.

through Finney's email correspondences with Nakamoto and concluded that he was not the cryptocurrency's creator. Finney died on August 28, 2014, after a battle with Amyotrophic Lateral Sclerosis (ALS), and was **cryopreserved** by the Alcor Life Extension Foundation.

Nick Szabo

Nick Szabo is a legal scholar, computer scientist, and cryptographer. He is best known for creating the concept of **smart contracts** in 1996. In 2010, Satoshi Nakamoto wrote that Bitcoin was partly an implementation of Nick Szabo's 2005 bit gold proposal. Bit gold shared many similarities with Bitcoin including proof-of-work, a shared database of ownership records, and the ability to eliminate inflation. However, bit gold differed from Bitcoin in several ways. The most notable being that bit gold relied on servers to keep track of ownership records, while Bitcoin incorporates ownership onto a blockchain shared by all participants in the network. This opened up bit gold to the risk of an untrustworthy party controlling the majority of servers.

Dorian Nakamoto majored in physics at the California State Polytechnic University in Pomona. Prior to 2001, Dorian worked for various technology companies and defense contractors. Some of his work was on classified military projects.

Dorian Nakamoto

Dorian Nakamoto, born Satoshi Nakamoto, is a computer systems engineer and programmer. In 2014, an article from *Newsweek* claimed that Dorian was the creator of Bitcoin. One of the main arguments in the article pointed to Dorian's lack of employment in computer work during Bitcoin's early years. Dorian argued that he struggled to find work throughout that time, performing jobs as a labourer, polltaker, and substitute teacher.

During Dorian's struggle with the media, the message "I am not Dorian Nakamoto" was sent from an email account known to belong to Satoshi Nakamoto. If authentic, this would have been Satoshi's first appearance after a 3-year absence. Also, in an interview with *Forbes*, Hal Finney gave convincing reasons why Dorian could not be Satoshi. However, *Newsweek* has refused to retract, apologize, or compensate Dorian for the article. Soon after, the Bitcoin community came together to fundraise approximately 63 bitcoin to help Dorian. In recent years, Dorian attends Bitcoin conferences as an invited guest, sometimes sharing the same room with Nick Szabo.

Elon Musk

In 2017, a former employee of SpaceX wrote several key points that point to Elon Musk being the creator of Bitcoin. Musk wrote production-level internet software for Paypal, a company founded in 1998 that facilitates payments between parties through online transfers. He also has a firm grasp of C++, the coding language used to write Bitcoin's software. Musk wrote software used by Paypal using C++, and insisted that C++ be used at SpaceX as well.

Another point in favor of Musk being the creator of Bitcoin was his unusual silence on Bitcoin. Elon Musk usually offers an opinion on everything tech related, yet in the first several years of Bitcoin's existence he stayed relatively quiet on the subject. Musk has also publicly stated that he does not own any bitcoin. In 2009, Satoshi mined bitcoin in order to test and strengthen the network. The "Good Satoshi" principle hinges on Satoshi deleting the private keys to an estimated one million bitcoin that he mined and never spent. In 2020, Elon Musk began increasingly discussing Bitcoin online.

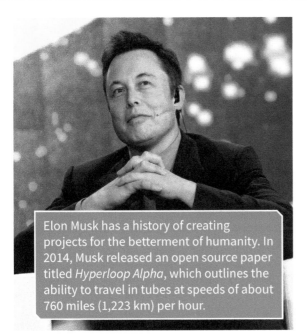

Elon Musk has a history of creating projects for the betterment of humanity. In 2014, Musk released an open source paper titled *Hyperloop Alpha*, which outlines the ability to travel in tubes at speeds of about 760 miles (1,223 km) per hour.

The former SpaceX employee also pointed out that Musk thinks of global solutions to large-scale problems. He founded SpaceX as a way to make humanity into a multiplanetary species, created Tesla Motors to reduce pollution with sustainable energy, and established The Boring Company to avoid traffic congestion. Similarly, Bitcoin was the solution to the 2008 financial crisis, solving a lack of trust in the banking system. While Musk has always denied being Bitcoin's creator, on February 8, 2021, Tesla Motors announced that it had purchased $1.5 billion in bitcoin.

The National Security Agency

A popular conspiracy theory is that the U.S. National Security Agency (NSA) created Bitcoin. This argument is based on the vast number of crytographers who are employed by the NSA, and that the complexity of creating Bitcoin must have involved a group effort. It also hinges on the idea that the U.S. government may want to one day replace the U.S. dollar with a digital currency, and that Bitcoin was set-up as a test-run. Proponents of this argument point to Bitcoin's use of

SHA-256 for mining and cryptographic key generation. Since SHA-256 was developed by the NSA, it has been suggested that they built a **backdoor** in the code that allows the agency to mathematically create a private key for any public key in existence. If this were possible, the NSA could theoretically forge any bitcoin transaction and essentially take control of the network. However, in the years since 2001, when SHA-256 was first publicly available, no one has been able to find a back-door, and there is no evidence to support the speculation that a back-door exists.

Revealing previously private personal information about individuals on the internet can have dire consequences. Dorian Nakamoto had his privacy taken away from him by an irresponsible media story. And Craig Write's story serves as a warning about the unpredictable steps that governments will take in response to a public doxing by the media. While the true identity of Nakamoto may never be known, cypherpunks are usually in agreement on two key points. Firstly, the privacy of the real Satoshi Nakamoto should be respected. Secondly, the decentralization of the Bitcoin network has made it impossible for the creator or creators of Bitcoin to shut the system down.

In 1997, the NSA published a paper titled *How to Make a Mint: the Cryptography of Anonymous Electronic Cash*. The paper examines how financial transactions can be made using a peer-to-peer network.

Bitcoin Around the World

Bitcoin has been used around the world since it was first created in 2009. Over time, different groups have helped to facilitate the use of bitcoin for the payment of goods and services. Today, Bitcoin users rely on these groups to help develop the thriving electronic currency so that it can be used for decades to come.

THE BITCOIN FOUNDATION
SAN FRANSISCO, CALIFORNIA

Founded in 2012, The Bitcoin Foundation is the largest and oldest cryptocurrency advocacy group in the world. The non-profit organization helps promote the development of Bitcoin technology and its adoption by the media and general public. Members of The Bitcoin Foundation regularly interact with lawmakers around the world to positively impact the direction of future cryptocurrency **legislation**.

BITPAY
ATLANTA, GEORGIA

BitPay is a global Bitcoin payment service provider that was founded in 2011. BitPay enables merchants to accept bitcoin in payment for transactions, while automatically converting the cryptocurrency into one of 30 different international currencies. This safety from Bitcoin price volatility, as well as transactions being non-reversible, make BitPay popular for merchants who process international transactions.

North America

Atlantic Ocean

Pacific Ocean

South America

Legend
- City
- Land
- Ocean

0   2,000 miles

0   4,000 kilometers

N

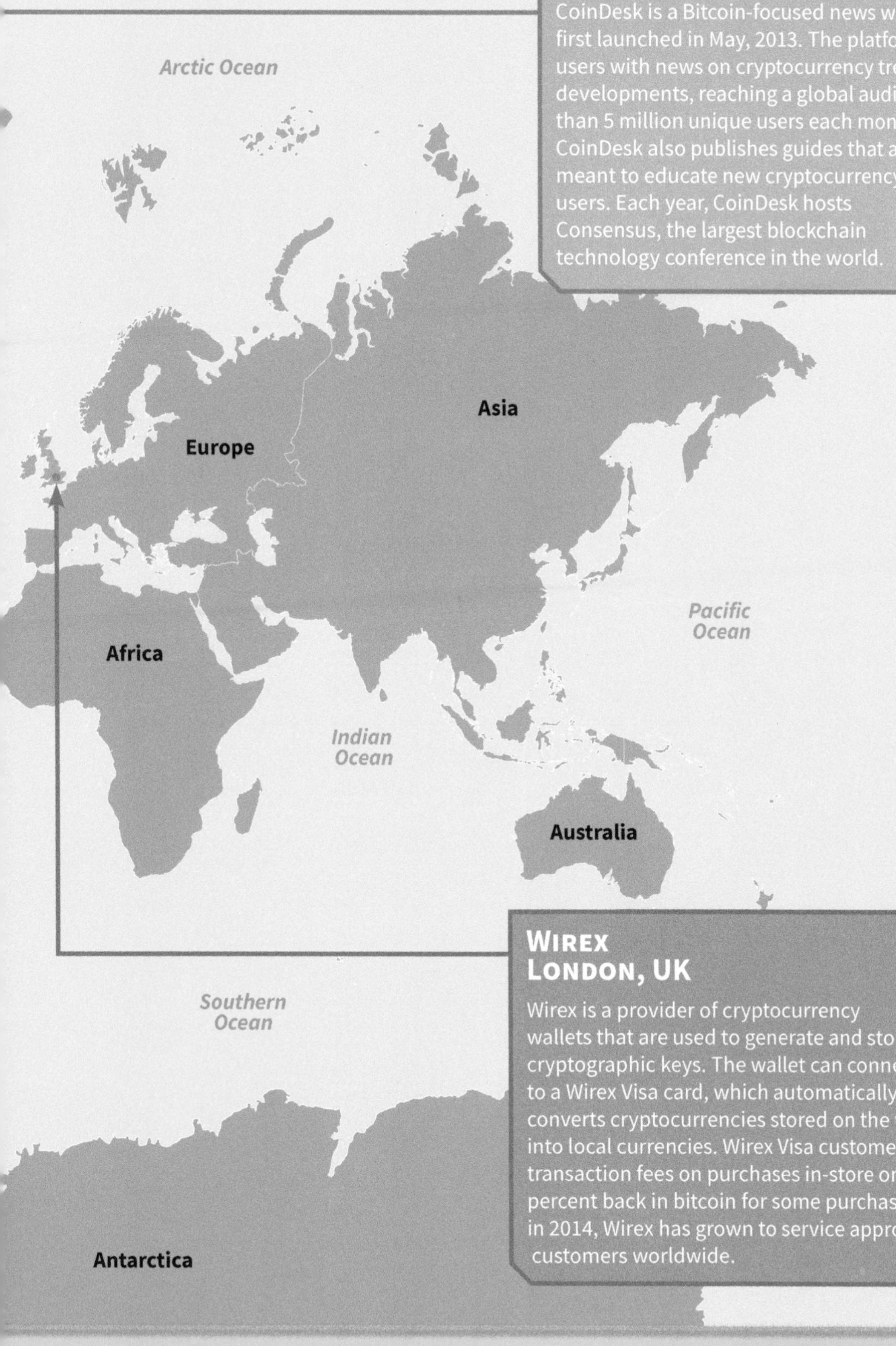

Arctic Ocean

CoinDesk
New York, NY

CoinDesk is a Bitcoin-focused news website that first launched in May, 2013. The platform provides users with news on cryptocurrency trends and developments, reaching a global audience of more than 5 million unique users each month. CoinDesk also publishes guides that are meant to educate new cryptocurrency users. Each year, CoinDesk hosts Consensus, the largest blockchain technology conference in the world.

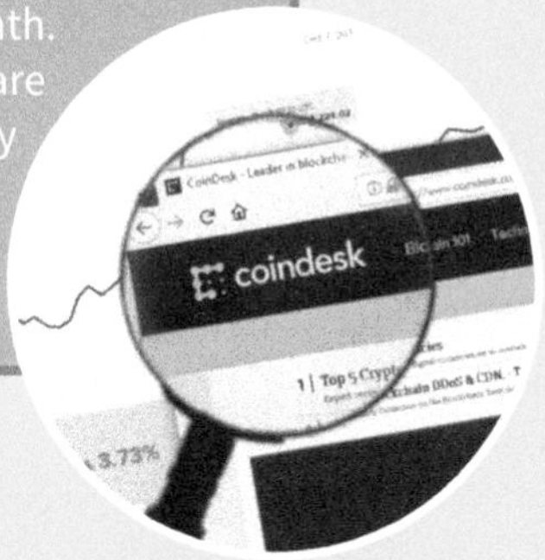

Asia

Europe

Africa

Pacific Ocean

Indian Ocean

Australia

Southern Ocean

Wirex
London, UK

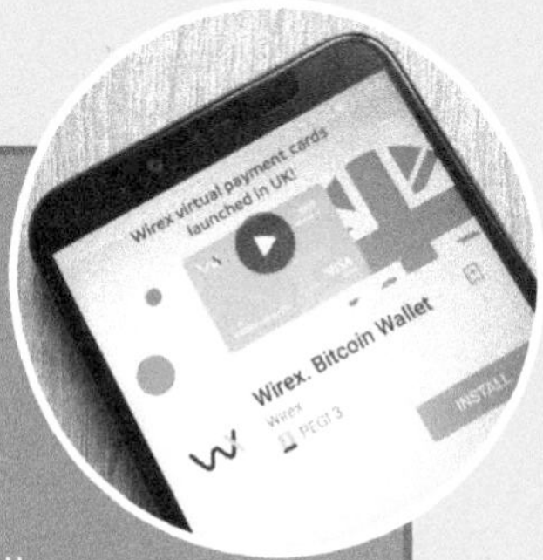

Wirex is a provider of cryptocurrency wallets that are used to generate and store cryptographic keys. The wallet can connect to a Wirex Visa card, which automatically converts cryptocurrencies stored on the wallet into local currencies. Wirex Visa customers do not pay transaction fees on purchases in-store or online and receive 0.5 percent back in bitcoin for some purchases. First established in 2014, Wirex has grown to service approximately 2 million customers worldwide.

Antarctica

Timeline of Bitcoin

2008 August 18 The bitcoin.org domain is registered at anonymousspeech.com, a site that allows users to anonymously register domain names.

2008 October 31 Satoshi Nakamoto publishes *Bitcoin: A Peer-to-Peer Electronic Cash System* to a cryptography mailing list called metzdowd.com.

2009 January 9 Bitcoin Version 0.1 is released. It was compiled through Microsoft's Visual Studio for Windows.

2009 January 12 Satoshi Nakamoto tests the Bitcoin network by sending 10 coins to Hal Finney. Finney becomes the first person in history to receive a Bitcoin transaction.

↓ **2010 May 22** Programmer Laszlo Hanyecz pays 10,000 bitcoins for two pizzas. This becomes the first transaction for goods on the Bitcoin network.

2010 November 6 The market valuation of bitcoin exceeds $1 million.

2010 December 8 The first mobile bitcoin transaction occurs using a program called bitcoind.

↑ **2011 April 23** Satoshi Nakamoto leaves Bitcoin, telling his successor Gavin Andresen that he has moved on to other things.

2011 May 16 *TIME* magazine publishes an article about Bitcoin, *Online Cash Bitcoin Could Challenge Governments, Banks*.

2011 August 20 The first Bitcoin Conference and World Expo is held in New York City.

2011 September Charlie Shrem founds BitInstant, allowing customers to purchase and make purchases with bitcoin at more than 7,000 locations.

2013 March 28 The total bitcoin market valuation passes $1 billion after Cameron Winklevoss places a market buy order on Mt. Gox, a Bitcoin exchange in Tokyo, Japan.

↑ **2013 October 1** Ross Ulbricht is arrested by the FBI for operating a black market website called the Silk Road, where bitcoin was the main form of payment.

↑ **2013 October 29** Robocoin launches the first bitcoin ATM in the world. It is placed in a Waves coffee shop in Vancouver, Canada.

2014 January Overstock.com becomes the first major online retailer to accept bitcoin.

2014 February 24 Mt. Gox suspends all bitcoin trading, claiming that 744,408 bitcoin were stolen by hackers.

2015 January 26 Coinbase becomes the first regulated bitcoin exchange in the U.S.

2015 February 23 Thaddeus Dryja and Joseph Poon publish the Lightning Network whitepaper.

2015 December Microsoft begins accepting bitcoin payments.

2016 December *Ledger*, published at the University of Pittsburgh, becomes the first peer-reviewed academic journal covering cryptocurrency and blockchain technology.

2017 October 8 Andreas Antonopoulos publishes Mastering Bitcoin, a programming textbook for developers.

2017 August 1 Bitcoin Cash, supported by Roger Ver, is created as a spin-off of Bitcoin. The cryptocurrency is not affiliated with Bitcoin even though it shares its name.

2017 August 23 Segregated Witness (SegWit) is activated in Bitcoin's software.

2017 October 20 Bitcoin's market valuation exceeds $100 billion.

2018 January Software developer Alex Bosworth is the first person to complete a transaction on the Lightning Network. He pays his phone bill through Bitrefill.

2020 July Banks in the United States can now hold bitcoin for their clients.

↑ **2020 September** Twitter CEO Jack Dorsey says that "Bitcoin is the future of Twitter." Dorsey had previously suggested that Bitcoin "has the potential to become the world's sole currency by 2030."

2020 October PayPal announces that it would allow users to buy and sell bitcoin on its platform.

2021 February 8 Tesla Motors announces in an SEC filing that it has invested $1.5 billion into Bitcoin, and confirmed plans to accept bitcoin for its products.

2021 February 19 The total bitcoin market valuation passes $1 trillion.

Activities

1. SEND A SECRET MESSAGE

In the 1980s, cypherpunks revolutionized the way in which people could send and receive private messages on the internet using Pretty Good Privacy (PGP). This technology is still used today to send messages online. Follow the steps below to use PGP to send a secret message to a friend.

1. Visit https://webencrypt.org/openpgpjs/. On the website, click on GENERATE PGP KEYS to create a public and private key pair. Have a friend to do the same. Save these keys in a safe place.

2. Send your public key to your friend and have your friend send his or her public key to you.

3. Next, click on ENCRYPT A MESSAGE. Write a secret message to encrypt in the YOUR MESSAGE field. Then, enter your friend's public key in the OUR PUBLIC KEY field and select ENCRYPT. Have your friend follow the same steps to have your friend encrypt a secret message, but have him or her use your public key in the Encryption field.

4. Copy and paste the encrypted message from the YOUR MESSAGE field, and email it to each other.

5. To decrypt your friend's message, select DECRYPT A MESSAGE. Paste the encrypted message in the YOUR ENCRYPTED MESSAGE field. Then, paste your private key in the YOUR PRIVATE KEY field and click DECRYPT MESSAGE. The encrypted message will automatically decode into readable text. Have your friend do the same using your private key and encrypted message.

For added security, find a downloadable PGP generator, and disconnect from the internet while generating your keys.

2. CREATE BITCOIN KEYS

Create public and private Bitcoin keys using a website such as https://www.bitaddress.org. Shake your mouse to help generate random numbers for your keys. Print or save these keys in a safe place. Your public key can be shared with other people. This is your Bitcoin address, and is used by other people to send you bitcoin. Never share your private key with anyone. You can unlock your funds at any time using your private key. Many security experts recommend disconnecting from the internet when generating private keys.

3. TURN TEXT INTO A SHA-256 HASH

Create a SHA-256 hash from a website such as http://passwordsgenerator.net/sha256-hash-generator/. Enter the text you would like to hash, such as your name, and select GENERATE. What happens to the hash if you add one letter to the end of your name? Can you come up with a nonce value that will add one or two leading zeros to the hash of your name?

Review

1 What is the alias of the person or persons who created Bitcoin?

2 What are the four pillars of Bitcoin?

3 What currency was legal tender in New England between 1637 and 1661?

4 What encryption software was used for the first secure internet purchase?

5 When Digicash's cyberbucks failed, what did it demonstrate to cypherpunks?

6 What hashing function converts data into a string of 64 characters?

7 What concept makes the blockchain immutable?

8 What is the first Bitcoin block known as?

9 What do miners add to the end of each block to create zeroes at the beginning of a hash?

10 What acts as links between blocks in the blockchain?

11 How often does the Bitcoin network adjust mining difficulty levels?

12 By what year are all 21 million bitcoin units predicted to have been created?

13 What new layer in Bitcoin's architecture will allow small Bitcoin transactions to take place outside of the regular blockchain?

14 Who received the first Bitcoin transaction from Satoshi Nakamoto on January 12, 2009?

15 Which group interacts with lawmakers to positively impact the direction of future cryptocurrency legislation around the world?

Answers: 1. Satoshi Nakamoto **2.** a peer-to-peer network, consensus rules, the blockchain, and proof-of-work **3.** Wampum **4.** Pretty Good Privacy (PGP) **5.** A centralized currency was prone to failure **6.** SHA-256 **7.** proof-of-work **8.** the Genesis Block **9.** a nonce **10.** hashes **11.** every 2016 blocks, which takes about two weeks **12.** 2140 **13.** the Lightning Network **14.** Hal Finney **15.** The Bitcoin Foundation

Appendix

THE BITCOIN WHITEPAPER BY
SATOSHI NAKAMOTO

Bitcoin: A Peer-to-Peer Electronic Cash System

Satoshi Nakamoto
satoshin@gmx.com
www.bitcoin.org

ABSTRACT. A purely peer-to-peer version of electronic cash would allow online payments to be sent directly from one party to another without going through a financial institution. Digital signatures provide part of the solution, but the main benefits are lost if a trusted third party is still required to prevent double-spending. We propose a solution to the double-spending problem using a peer-to-peer network. The network timestamps transactions by hashing them into an ongoing chain of hash-based proof-of-work, forming a record that cannot be changed without redoing the proof-of-work. The longest chain not only serves as proof of the sequence of events witnessed, but proof that it came from the largest pool of CPU power. As long as a majority of CPU power is controlled by nodes that are not cooperating to attack the network, they'll generate the longest chain and outpace attackers. The network itself requires minimal structure. Messages are broadcast on a best effort basis, and nodes can leave and rejoin the network at will, accepting the longest proof-of-work chain as proof of what happened while they were gone.

1. INTRODUCTION

Commerce on the Internet has come to rely almost exclusively on financial institutions serving as trusted third parties to process electronic payments. While the system works well enough for most transactions, it still suffers from the inherent weaknesses of the trust based model. Completely non-reversible transactions are not really possible, since financial institutions cannot avoid mediating disputes. The cost of mediation increases transaction costs, limiting the minimum practical transaction size and cutting off the possibility for small casual transactions, and there is a broader cost in the loss of ability to make non-reversible payments for nonreversible services. With the possibility of reversal, the need for trust spreads. Merchants must be wary of their customers, hassling them for more information than they would otherwise need. A certain percentage of fraud is accepted as unavoidable. These costs and payment uncertainties can be avoided in person by using physical currency, but no mechanism exists to make payments over a communications channel without a trusted party.

What is needed is an electronic payment system based on cryptographic proof instead of trust, allowing any two willing parties to transact directly with each other without the need for a trusted third party. Transactions that are computationally impractical to reverse would protect sellers from fraud, and routine escrow mechanisms could easily be implemented to protect buyers. In this paper, we propose a solution to the double-spending problem using a peer-to-peer distributed timestamp server to generate computational proof of the chronological order of transactions. The system is secure as long as honest nodes collectively control more CPU power than any cooperating group of attacker nodes.

2. TRANSACTIONS

We define an electronic coin as a chain of digital signatures. Each owner transfers the coin to the next by digitally signing a hash of the previous transaction and the public key of the next owner and adding these to the end of the coin. A payee can verify the signatures to verify the chain of ownership.

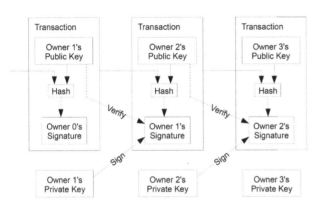

The problem of course is the payee can't verify that one of the owners did not double-spend the coin. A common solution is to introduce a trusted central authority, or mint, that checks every transaction for double spending. After each transaction, the coin must be returned to the mint to issue a new coin, and only coins issued directly from the mint are trusted not to be double-spent. The problem with this solution is that the fate of the entire money system depends on the company running the mint, with every transaction having to go through them, just like a bank.

We need a way for the payee to know that the previous owners did not sign any earlier transactions. For our purposes, the earliest transaction is the one that counts, so we don't care about later attempts to double-spend. The only way to confirm the absence of a transaction is to be aware of all transactions. In the mint based model, the mint was aware of all transactions and decided which arrived first. To accomplish this without a trusted party, transactions must be publicly announced [1], and we need a system for participants to agree on a single history of the order in which they were received. The payee needs proof that at the time of each transaction, the majority of nodes agreed it was the first received.

3. TIMESTAMP SERVER

The solution we propose begins with a timestamp server. A timestamp server works by taking a hash of a block of items to be timestamped and widely publishing the hash, such as in a newspaper or Usenet post [2-5]. The timestamp proves that the data must have existed at the time, obviously, in order to get into the hash. Each timestamp includes the previous timestamp in its hash, forming a chain, with each additional timestamp reinforcing the ones before it.

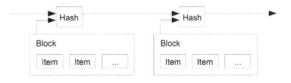

4. PROOF-OF-WORK

To implement a distributed timestamp server on a peer-to-peer basis, we will need to use a proofof-work system similar to Adam Back's Hashcash [6], rather than newspaper or Usenet posts. The proof-of-work involves scanning for a value that when hashed, such as with SHA-256, the hash begins with a number of zero bits. The average work required is exponential in the number of zero bits required and can be verified by executing a single hash.

For our timestamp network, we implement the proof-of-work by incrementing a nonce in the block until a value is found that gives the block's hash the required zero bits. Once the CPU effort has been expended to make it satisfy the proof-of-work, the block cannot be changed without redoing the work. As later blocks are chained after it, the work to change the block would include redoing all the blocks after it.

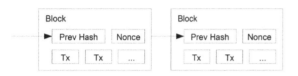

The proof-of-work also solves the problem of determining representation in majority decision making. If the majority were based on one-IP-address-one-vote, it could be subverted by anyone able to allocate many IPs. Proof-of-work is essentially one-CPU-one-vote. The majority decision is represented by the longest chain, which has the greatest proof-of-work effort invested in it. If a majority of CPU power is controlled by honest nodes, the honest chain will grow the fastest and outpace any competing chains. To modify a past block, an attacker would have to redo the proof-of-work of the block and all blocks after it and then catch up with and surpass the work of the honest nodes. We will show later that the probability of a slower attacker catching up diminishes exponentially as subsequent blocks are added.

To compensate for increasing hardware speed and varying interest in running nodes over time, the proof-of-work difficulty is determined by a moving average targeting an average number of blocks per hour. If they're generated too fast, the difficulty increases.

5. NETWORK
The steps to run the network are as follows:

1) New transactions are broadcast to all nodes.
2) Each node collects new transactions into a block.
3) Each node works on finding a difficult proof-of-work for its block.
4) When a node finds a proof-of-work, it broadcasts the block to all nodes.
5) Nodes accept the block only if all transactions in it are valid and not already spent.
6) Nodes express their acceptance of the block by working on creating the next block in the chain, using the hash of the accepted block as the previous hash.

Nodes always consider the longest chain to be the correct one and will keep working on extending it. If two nodes broadcast different versions of the next block simultaneously, some nodes may receive one or the other first. In that case, they work on the first one they received, but save the other branch in case it becomes longer. The tie will be broken when the next proofof-work is found and one branch becomes longer; the nodes that were working on the other branch will then switch to the longer one.

New transaction broadcasts do not necessarily need to reach all nodes. As long as they reach many nodes, they will get into a block before long. Block broadcasts are also tolerant of dropped messages. If a node does not receive a block, it will request it when it receives the next block and realizes it missed one.

6. INCENTIVE

By convention, the first transaction in a block is a special transaction that starts a new coin owned by the creator of the block. This adds an incentive for nodes to support the network, and provides a way to initially distribute coins into circulation, since there is no central authority to issue them. The steady addition of a constant of amount of new coins is analogous to gold miners expending resources to add gold to circulation. In our case, it is CPU time and electricity that is expended.

The incentive can also be funded with transaction fees. If the output value of a transaction is less than its input value, the difference is a transaction fee that is added to the incentive value of the block containing the transaction. Once a predetermined number of coins have entered circulation, the incentive can transition entirely to transaction fees and be completely inflation free.

The incentive may help encourage nodes to stay honest. If a greedy attacker is able to assemble more CPU power than all the honest nodes, he would have to choose between using it to defraud people by stealing back his payments, or using it to generate new coins. He ought to find it more profitable to play by the rules, such rules that favour him with more new coins than everyone else combined, than to undermine the system and the validity of his own wealth.

7. RECLAIMING DISK SPACE

Once the latest transaction in a coin is buried under enough blocks, the spent transactions before it can be discarded to save disk space. To facilitate this without breaking the block's hash, transactions are

hashed in a Merkle Tree [7][2][5], with only the root included in the block's hash. Old blocks can then be compacted by stubbing off branches of the tree. The interior hashes do not need to be stored.

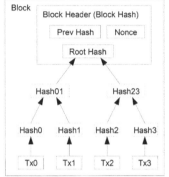 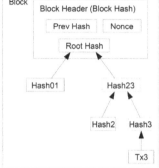

Transactions Hashed in a Merkle Tree　　After Pruning Tx0-2 from the Block

A block header with no transactions would be about 80 bytes. If we suppose blocks are generated every 10 minutes, 80 bytes * 6 * 24 * 365 = 4.2MB per year. With computer systems typically selling with 2GB of RAM as of 2008, and Moore's Law predicting current growth of 1.2GB per year, storage should not be a problem even if the block headers must be kept in memory.

8. SIMPLIFIED PAYMENT VERIFICATION

It is possible to verify payments without running a full network node. A user only needs to keep a copy of the block headers of the longest proof-of-work chain, which he can get by querying network nodes until he's convinced he has the longest chain, and obtain the Merkle branch linking the transaction to the block it's timestamped in. He can't check the transaction for himself, but by linking it to a place in the chain, he can see that a network node has accepted it, and blocks added after it further confirm the network has accepted it.

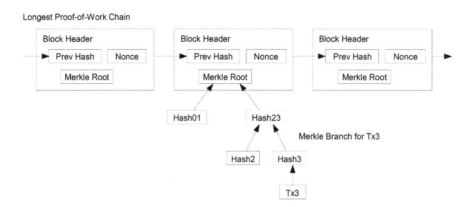

Longest Proof-of-Work Chain

It should be noted that fan-out, where a transaction depends on several transactions, and those transactions depend on many more, is not a problem here. There is never the need to extract a complete standalone copy of a transaction's history.

As such, the verification is reliable as long as honest nodes control the network, but is more vulnerable if the network is overpowered by an attacker. While network nodes can verify transactions for themselves, the simplified method can be fooled by an attacker's fabricated transactions for as long as the attacker can continue to overpower the network. One strategy to protect against this would be to accept alerts from network nodes when they detect an invalid block, prompting the user's software to download the full block and alerted transactions to confirm the inconsistency. Businesses that receive frequent payments will probably still want to run their own nodes for more independent security and quicker verification.

9. COMBINING AND SPLITTING VALUE

Although it would be possible to handle coins individually, it would be unwieldy to make a separate transaction for every cent in a transfer. To allow value to be split and combined, transactions contain multiple inputs and outputs. Normally there will be either a single input from a larger previous transaction or multiple inputs combining smaller amounts, and at most two outputs: one for the payment, and one returning the change, if any, back to the sender.

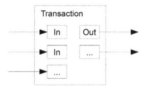

It should be noted that fan-out, where a transaction depends on several transactions, and those transactions depend on many more, is not a problem here. There is never the need to extract a complete standalone copy of a transaction's history.

10. PRIVACY

The traditional banking model achieves a level of privacy by limiting access to information to the parties involved and the trusted third party. The necessity to announce all transactions publicly precludes this method, but privacy can still be maintained by breaking the flow of information in another place: by keeping public keys anonymous. The public can see that someone is sending an amount to someone else, but without information linking the transaction to anyone. This is similar to the level of information released by stock exchanges,

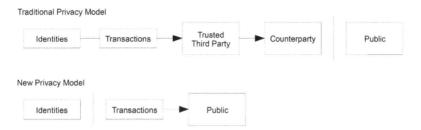

Traditional Privacy Model

Identities ---- Transactions ➤ Trusted Third Party ➤ Counterparty | Public

New Privacy Model

Identities | Transactions ➤ Public

where the time and size of individual trades, the "tape", is made public, but without telling who the parties were.

As an additional firewall, a new key pair should be used for each transaction to keep them from being linked to a common owner. Some linking is still unavoidable with multi-input transactions, which necessarily reveal that their inputs were owned by the same owner. The risk is that if the owner of a key is revealed, linking could reveal other transactions that belonged to the same owner.

11. CALCULATIONS

We consider the scenario of an attacker trying to generate an alternate chain faster than the honest chain. Even if this is accomplished, it does not throw the system open to arbitrary changes, such as creating value out of thin air or taking money that never belonged to the attacker. Nodes are not going to accept an invalid transaction as payment, and honest nodes will never accept a block containing them. An attacker can only try to change one of his own transactions to take back money he recently spent.

The race between the honest chain and an attacker chain can be characterized as a Binomial Random Walk. The success event is the honest chain being extended by one block, increasing its lead by +1, and the failure event is the attacker's chain being extended by one block, reducing the gap by -1.

The probability of an attacker catching up from a given deficit is analogous to a Gambler's Ruin problem. Suppose a gambler with unlimited credit starts at a deficit and plays potentially an infinite number of trials to try to reach breakeven. We can calculate the probability he ever reaches breakeven, or that an attacker ever catches up with the honest chain, as follows [8]:

p = probability an honest node finds the next block

q = probability the attacker finds the next block

q_z = probability the attacker will ever catch up from z blocks behind

$$q_z = \begin{cases} 1 & \text{if } p \leq q \\ (q/p)^z & \text{if } p > q \end{cases}$$

Given our assumption that p > q, the probability drops exponentially as the number of blocks the attacker has to catch up with increases. With the odds against him, if he doesn't make a lucky lunge forward early on, his chances become vanishingly small as he falls further behind.

We now consider how long the recipient of a new transaction needs to wait before being sufficiently certain the sender can't change the transaction. We assume the sender is an attacker who wants to make the recipient believe he paid him for a while, then switch it to pay back to himself after some time has passed. The receiver will be alerted when that happens, but the sender hopes it will be too late.

The receiver generates a new key pair and gives the public key to the sender shortly before signing. This prevents the sender from preparing a chain of blocks ahead of time by working on it continuously until he is lucky enough to get far enough ahead, then executing the transaction at that moment. Once the transaction is sent, the dishonest sender starts working in secret on a parallel chain containing an alternate version of his transaction.

The recipient waits until the transaction has been added to a block and z blocks have been linked after it. He doesn't know the exact amount of progress the attacker has made, but assuming the honest blocks took the average expected time per block, the attacker's potential progress will be a Poisson distribution with expected value:

$$\lambda = z \frac{q}{p}$$

To get the probability the attacker could still catch up now, we multiply the Poisson density for each amount of progress he could have made by the probability he could catch up from that point:

$$\sum_{k=0}^{\infty} \frac{\lambda^k e^{-\lambda}}{k!} \cdot \left\{ \begin{array}{ll} (q/p)^{(z-k)} & if \ k \le z \\ 1 & if \ k > z \end{array} \right\}$$

Rearranging to avoid summing the infinite tail of the distribution...

$$1 - \sum_{k=0}^{z} \frac{\lambda^k e^{-\lambda}}{k!} \left(1 - (q/p)^{(z-k)}\right)$$

Converting to C code...

```c
#include <math.h>
double AttackerSuccessProbability(double q,
int z)
{
    double p = 1.0 - q;
    double lambda = z * (q / p);
    double sum = 1.0;
    int i, k;
    for (k = 0; k <= z; k++)
    {
        double poisson = exp(-lambda);
        for (i = 1; i <= k; i++)
            poisson *= lambda / i;
        sum -= poisson * (1 - pow(q / p, z -
k));
    }
    return sum;
}
```

Running some results, we can see the probability drop off exponentially with z.

```
q=0.1
z=0  P=1.0000000
z=1  P=0.2045873
z=2  P=0.0509779
z=3  P=0.0131722
z=4  P=0.0034552
z=5  P=0.0009137
z=6  P=0.0002428
z=7  P=0.0000647
z=8  P=0.0000173
z=9  P=0.0000046
z=10 P=0.0000012

q=0.3
z=0  P=1.0000000
z=5  P=0.1773523
z=10 P=0.0416605
z=15 P=0.0101008
z=20 P=0.0024804
z=25 P=0.0006132
z=30 P=0.0001522
z=35 P=0.0000379
z=40 P=0.0000095
z=45 P=0.0000024
z=50 P=0.0000006
```

Solving for P less than 0.1%...

```
P < 0.001
q=0.10  z=5
q=0.15  z=8
q=0.20  z=11
q=0.25  z=15
q=0.30  z=24
q=0.35  z=41
q=0.40  z=89
q=0.45  z=340
```

12. CONCLUSION

We have proposed a system for electronic transactions without relying on trust. We started with the usual framework of coins made from digital signatures, which provides strong control of ownership, but is incomplete without a way to prevent double-spending. To solve this, we proposed a peer-to-peer network using proof-of-work to record a public history of transactions that quickly becomes computationally impractical for an attacker to change if honest nodes control a majority of CPU power. The network is robust in its unstructured simplicity. Nodes work all at once with little coordination. They do not need to be identified, since messages are not routed to any particular place and only need to be delivered on a best effort basis. Nodes can leave and rejoin the network at will, accepting the proof-of-work chain as proof of what happened while they were gone. They vote with their CPU power, expressing their acceptance of valid blocks by working on extending them and rejecting invalid blocks by refusing to work on them. Any needed rules and incentives can be enforced with this consensus mechanism.

REFERENCES

[1] W. Dai, "b-money," http://www.weidai.com/bmoney.txt, 1998.

[2] H. Massias, X.S. Avila, and J.-J. Quisquater, "Design of a secure timestamping service with minimal trust requirements," In 20th Symposium on Information Theory in the Benelux, May 1999.

[3] S. Haber, W.S. Stornetta, "How to time-stamp a digital document," In Journal of Cryptology, vol 3, no 2, pages 99-111, 1991.

[4] D. Bayer, S. Haber, W.S. Stornetta, "Improving the efficiency and reliability of digital time-stamping," In Sequences II: Methods in Communication, Security and Computer Science, pages 329-334, 1993.

[5] S. Haber, W.S. Stornetta, "Secure names for bit-strings," In Proceedings of the 4th ACM Conference on Computer and Communications Security, pages 28-35, April 1997.

[6] A. Back, "Hashcash - a denial of service counter-measure," http://www.hashcash.org/papers/hashcash.pdf, 2002.

[7] R.C. Merkle, "Protocols for public key cryptosystems," In Proc. 1980 Symposium on Security and Privacy, IEEE Computer Society, pages 122-133, April 1980.

[8] W. Feller, "An introduction to probability theory and its applications," 1957.

LICENSE

This whitepaper was published in October 2008 by Satoshi Nakamoto. It was later (2009) added as supporting documentation to the Bitcoin software and carries the same MIT license. It has been reproduced in this book, without modification other than formatting, under the terms of the MIT license:

IMAGE CREDITS

Page 5 (Coinbase): 24K-Production / Shutterstock.com
Page 5 (Bitcoin ATM): Victor Babenko / Shutterstock.com
Page 10 (Philip Zimmermann): Image courtesy of Philip Zimmermann
Page 11 (David Chaum): Horacio Villalobos / Getty Images
Page 12 (*Wired* magazine): Larry Dyer
Page 13 (Vintage computer): Tinxi / Shutterstock.com
Page 13 (Milton Friedman): Image courtesy of The Friedman Foundation for Educational Choice
Page 14 (Bangladesh street): Tarzan9280 / istockphoto.com
Page 17 (Adam Back): Image courtesy of Adam Back
Page 19 (Portland, Oregon): DaveAlan / istockphoto.com
Page 22 (Argentina) Diego O. Galeano / Shutterstock.com
Page 25 (Claus Schnorr) Konrad Jacobs / Creative Commons Attribution-Share Alike 2.0 licence
Page 30 (Dorian Nakamoto): Kevin McGovern / Shutterstock.com
Page 30 (Hacker): Gualtiero Boffi / Shutterstock.com
Page 31 (Elon Musk): John Smith Williams / Shutterstock.com
Page 31 (NSA): Brooks Kraft / Getty Images
Page 32 (Bitpay): Grey82 / Shutterstock.com
Page 33 (Wirex): Piotr Swat / Shutterstock.com
Page 33 (Coindesk): dennizn / Shutterstock.com
Page 35 (Hardware wallet): Quinten Jacobs / Shutterstock.com
Page 42 (Gavin Andresen): Handout / Getty Images
Page 35 (Jack Dorsey): Frederic Legrand - COMEO / Shutterstock.com

Note from the Author: For the second edition of this book I would like to include a photo of Hal Finney as his contribution to cryptography and Bitcoin is exceptional. If you know how to contact the estate of Hal Finney, please let them know about this request.

CONTACT THE AUTHOR

The only way to contact me is to leave a comment in the review section on any Amazon website. I acknowledge that the subject matter of *Introduction to Bitcoin* is complex, and that I might have made errors in my explanations. I would be greatful if readers could jot down any constructive feedback and leave it in the review section on Amazon. I would also love to hear what aspects of this book you found useful or entertaining (these stories are what fuel me as a writer). I will read all comments, and will update future editions of this book based on your feedback.

ACKNOWLEDGEMENTS

The author would like to thank Adam Back and Philip Zimmermann for permission to use their images. The author would also like to thank Andreas Antonopoulos for producing a vast resource of educational content, which was instrumental in the creation of this book.

Key Words

anonymous: of unknown origin

backdoor: a method of bypassing a computer program's authentication or encryption systems

blockchain: a system in which a record of transactions are maintained across several computers linked together in a peer-to-peer network

centralized: the control of an activity by a single authority

colonists: settlers ruled by a parent nation

commodity: a basic or useful good used in commerce

computational: a calculation that follows a predetermined set of rules to solve a problem

counterfeit: an imitation of something valuable that is used to deceive others

cryopreserved: preserving cells and tissue through freezing

cryptographer: someone who studies or practices sending secure communications to third-parties

cypherpunks: activists that use cryptography as a means of enacting social and political change

decentralized: the distribution of administrative powers to many widespread parties

elliptic-curve: a plane algebraic curve that does not intersect itself

encryption: the process of encoding information that can only be deciphered by an authorized party

friendly fraud: when a consumer receives goods from an online credit card purchase and requests a refund from the credit card provider

geosynchronous: an orbital period that matches Earth's rotation on its axis

hard fork: occurs when existing rules are loosened or eliminated.

immutable: something that, once created, cannot be changed

inflation: when the price of goods increases while the value of a currency decreases

joules: a unit of energy measurement

ledger: a book or computer file that is used to record economic transactions

legislation: a law or laws made by a government

Linux: a computer operating system released in 1991

mining pool: a group of bitcoin miners that combine their computational resources and split bitcoin rewards

mnemonic phrase: a group words, often 12 or more, created when a new cryptocurrency wallet is made

multiverse: a hypothetical group of multiple universes

nodes: a computer connected to other computers which follows rules and shares information

nonce: a random number that is typically used in a cryptographic authentication protocol

open source: a software development model that encourages open collaboration between peers

phishing: a fraudulent attempt to obtain sensitive information or data, such as usernames and passwords

pseudonym: a fictitious name that is used to conceal an identity

reparations: making amends for causing an injury or injustice to others

server: a device or computer that manages resources on a network

smart contracts: computer protocols that enable the enforcement of a digital contract to self-execute

two-factor authentication: two forms of electronic verification are required to log-in to an account. Usually a password is combined with a code sent by text message

QR code: a type of matrix barcode which can be read by an imaging device such as a camera

Index

About the Author

My interest in Bitcoin began in 2017. I started researching this book in early 2018, and nearly completed writing it by the end of the summer. At this time I began asking people in the Bitcoin community for help with certain questions, or for permissions for photos. I am extremely grateful for the help I received from several individuals, including cypherpunks. However, after an unusual experience, I decided to protect my identity. The severety of the experience pushed me away from Bitcoin until I decided to have this book published in 2021. I genuinely hope that the knowledge in this textbook is valuable to the next generation of cypherpunks.

Sincerely,

David Ricardo

Proof of Identity

If someone claims to be David Ricardo, do not trust their claims without verification. A secure way to verify someone's identity is by receiving a message signed by a Bitcoin private key. Please do not accept any other method of verification for the identity of David Ricardo.

To verify my identity, you will need my Bitcoin address:

15sLRaSXwRezibCThtLuPrSQqFwdLMTX2n

Next, ask whoever is claiming to be David Ricardo to sign a particular message of your choosing. This circumvents a scenario where someone could be reposting a message that I have signed at an earlier date.

Then, you can verify my message using most Bitcoin wallets, or through an online verification tool such as: https://reinproject.org/bitcoin-signature-tool/#verify

Please do not send any bitcoin to the above address with any expectation that I will perform a particular service. Any funds received will be gratefully welcomed as a donation, and I will use these funds to continue to educate people about Bitcoin.

CPSIA information can be obtained
at www.ICGtesting.com
Printed in the USA
LVHW072255210521
688193LV00017B/1140